HABITUDES®

IMAGES
THAT FORM
LEADERSHIP
HABITS &
ATTITUDES

BY
DR TIM
ELMORE

This book is dedicated to all those who
are communicators and advocates for
agriculture, the people who ensure others
understand the priority of feeding the world
and who labor to accelerate that outcome.
They solve problems and serve people.
They are unsung heroes and leaders who
positively influence history.

PUBLISHED IN ATLANTA, GEORGIA BY GROWING LEADERS, INC.
(WWW.GROWINGLEADERS.COM)

ISBN: 978-0-9966970-1-9
PRINTED IN THE UNITED STATES OF AMERICA
LIBRARY OF CONGRESS CATALOGUING-IN-PUBLICATION DATA

TABLE OF CONTENTS

★

A WORD ABOUT IMAGES

We live in a culture rich with images. You grew up with photos, TV, movies, video, Facebook, MTV, Instagram and DVDs. We can't escape the power of a visual image…and most of us don't want to.

I've learned over my career that most of us are visual learners. We like to see a picture, not just hear a word. Author Leonard Sweet says that images are the language of the 21st century, not words. Some of the best communicators in history taught using the power of the metaphor and image—from Jesus Christ and His parables to Martin Luther King Jr. and his "I Have a Dream" speech during the Civil Rights movement. "The best leaders," writes Tom Peters, "…almost without exception and at every level, are master users of stories and symbols."

Why? Because pictures stick. We remember pictures long after words have left us. When we hear a speech, we often remember the stories from that speech, more than the lines used by the speaker, because they painted a picture inside of us. They communicate far more than mere words. In fact, words are helpful only as they conjure up a picture in our minds. Most of us think in pictures. If I say the word "elephant" to you, you don't picture the letters: e-l-e-p-h-a-n-t. You picture a big gray animal. Pictures are what we file away in our minds. They enable us to store huge volumes of information. There's an old phrase that has stood the test of time: A picture is worth a thousand words. It was while pursuing a college degree in commercial art that I recognized the power of images. Now I get to combine my love of leadership with the power of pictures. I trust they'll impact you profoundly as they have me.

Each image in this book represents a principle you can carry with you the rest of your life. They are truths I wish someone had told me before I entered my career. Most are simple, but each is profound if put into practice. They're all about the soft skills you need to succeed at work. In nationwide surveys, employers continue to reiterate that they're desperately looking for new professionals who possess "soft skills." Hard skills are important—abilities like computing, analyzing and strategic planning—but soft skills differentiate employees who have them: work ethic, great attitudes, teamwork, empathy and communication. For some, the step from a campus to a career feels like a cross-cultural experience. In the same way you feel a little out of place when you travel to a different country, the move from backpack to briefcase may seem like a journey to a foreign land with new values, people, language and customs. The book is designed to be a map to guide you, furnishing pictures to discuss with a community of people. It's part of a series I encourage you to go through in a group. Each picture contains layers of reality, and your discussion can go as deep as you allow it to go. It's a guide for your leadership journey.

Some sociologists describe this generation as EPIC: Experiential, Participatory, Image-rich and Connected. I agree. So each of these books provides you not only with an image, but a handful of discussion questions, a self-assessment and an exercise in which you can participate. Dive in and experience each one of them. My hope is that they become signposts that guide you, warn you, and inform you on your leadership journey.

Dr. Tim Elmore

FINDING OUR LEADERSHIP VOICE

We in agricultural education know the facts: FFA is the premier school-based, member-led youth organization. It provides transformational, life-changing experiences to future generations of agriculture, food and natural resources communicators and advocates who are driven by strong values, service to others and global purpose. Our members represent an investment in leadership for industry, public service and local communities.

Our challenge is to help others discover and appreciate these truths. That's why FFA is excited to offer this customized resource focused specifically on agricultural advocacy. *The Habitudes: The Art of Telling Our Story* was developed in partnership with our friends at Growing Leaders. By working with such innovative organizations, FFA continues to do what we do best—grow leaders, build communities and strengthen agriculture.

We understand the importance of providing compelling, relevant resources that equip FFA members to find their leadership voice. Each image in this book was carefully chosen and represents a foundational leadership principle. Our goal is that the images and lessons will prepare readers at all levels to be effective advocates in agriculture and other important areas of their lives.

Thanks for sharing with others your personal experiences and the FFA story of leadership, growth and career success. By doing so, we ensure a bright future for our industry and the organization we all know and love. We are FFA!

Joshua Bledsoe
Chief Operating Officer
National FFA Organization

IMAGE ONE
[The Half-Hearted Kamikaze]

The Half-Hearted Kamikaze

KAMIKAZE PILOTS ARE ONLY USEFUL IF THEY ARE COMMITTED TO THEIR MISSION. COMMUNICATORS AND ADVOCATES ARE THE SAME WAY. YOU CANNOT HAVE INVOLVEMENT WITHOUT COMMITMENT AND BE EFFECTIVE. IT GOES WITH THE TERRITORY.

I love this story of a kamikaze pilot who flew in World War II for the Japanese Air Force. He was interviewed by a newspaper reporter after returning from his fiftieth mission. The reporter asked the pilot if he wasn't a contradiction in terms. How can someone be a kamikaze pilot—whose mission is to fly into military bases and give up their life in the process—and still be alive after fifty missions?

"Well it's like this," the pilot responded. "I was very involved. Not very committed, but very involved."

I always smile when I think of this story. A true kamikaze pilot only flies on one mission. He gives his life for that one mission. He cannot be involved without being committed. There's no such thing as a half-hearted kamikaze. Commitment goes with the territory. And so it is with us. If we have any hope of being a successful person, much less an effective advocate, we must be committed. Communicators and advocates possess commitment. They cannot be involved without being committed. The rest of the world may enjoy involvement without commitment—but we cannot—as emerging communicators and advocates.

What's the difference between involvement and commitment? Just think about a pig and a chicken, after eating a ham and egg breakfast. The chicken was involved. The pig was committed!

The word "mediocre" was first used to describe rock (or mountain) climbers who were involved but not committed. The word literally means "middle of the rock." It was used to describe climbers who started a climb to the top but didn't finish. They stopped halfway. Ouch. Sound familiar?

Our schools and communities are filled with folks who are involved but not really committed. They want to keep all their options open, and often they don't make decisions until the last minute because a better opportunity may arise at the eleventh hour.

In fact, because our world offers us so many options, we tend to not commit ourselves because we don't want to narrow our focus. We want to do it all! The problem is, we can't do it all. Nearly every great leader in history accomplished something memorable because of a narrow focus and a great commitment to a cause. Even young leaders have figured this out and made their mark because they got committed.

Joan of Arc knew her life mission by the time she was fifteen years old. At seventeen, she led 3,000 French knights in battle. On one occasion, she told a military general, "I will lead the way over the wall." The general replied, "Not a man will follow you." Joan of Arc said, "I won't be looking back to see if they're following me."

At nineteen she was burned alive because she would not recant on her commitment to France. The British gave her a chance to regain her liberty if she would only change her allegiance, but she would not. In choosing to die at the stake she said, "Everyone gives their life for what they believe. Sometimes people believe in little or nothing and yet they give their life to that little or nothing. One life is all we have, and we live it, and then it's gone. But to give up what you are and to live without belief is more terrible than dying, even more terrible than dying young."

John Wesley founded the organization that later became the Methodist Church when he was seventeen. He could have done many other things. He was educated at Oxford and enjoyed horticulture, medicine, journalism, and politics. But he saw the great spiritual need of England during the 18th century and committed himself to spiritual renewal. He traveled over 250,000 miles on horseback, teaching and organizing churches for more than fifty years. Unlike Joan of Arc, Wesley died of old age, but not until his movement had impacted Great Britain. One history book reported that John Wesley almost single-handedly saved England from bloody revolution.

How Commitment Works

Today, many students talk about commitments they're going to make, but often fail to keep them. New Years resolutions last until February or March, at best. We say we believe in something or we make a promise—then we drift from it. Talk is cheap. Half-hearted kamikazes are a dime a dozen. The reason some people live such quality lives and possess such great influence is that they DO more than talk. They're committed to some ideals, and they live them out. They move from a "wish" to a "lifestyle" by surrendering to a cause along the way. There are phases we usually experience as we build commitment in our lives. It starts with an idea and ends with a conviction:

PHASE	DESCRIPTION

IDEAS: *We perceive an issue by the way we think about it. This involves our minds.*

OPINIONS: *We begin to express our preferences on that issue. This involves our emotions.*

BELIEFS: *We conclude where we stand on the issue. This involves both mind and emotions.*

COMMITMENTS: *We begin to act on our belief. This involves our mind, emotions and will.*

CONVICTIONS: *We are ready to die for our commitment. It now is a passion in our lives.*

Your dedication to a cause like agriculture advocacy will mean something when you act on it for an extended period of time. In the 2012 Census of Agriculture, the US Department of Agriculture reported that the average age of an American farmer is 58 years old. Our country needs young people to step into agriculture advocacy roles, and it will take a strong sense of commitment. When you become committed, you will notice something wonderful. The moment you make a commitment you will find all kinds of wisdom, energy, and resources at your disposal that weren't necessarily there before you committed yourself. Commitment opens up the floodgates to the resources you need—but they won't show up a moment too soon. Many of you want to see everything in place before getting committed. Unfortunately, you will never act if you wait for perfect conditions. That attitude can lead to being a half-hearted kamikaze. Others of you wait for a feeling before acting. You want to "feel" led to do something. Once again, you may be waiting for a while. *We are much more likely to act our way into a feeling, than we are to feel our way into action.* Get committed long enough, and eventually that commitment will become a conviction of which you will be very passionate.

TALK IT OVER

Even the most effective and hard-working agriculture leaders and advocates will face adversity and distractions. Developing a "strong muscle" of commitment gives you the extra energy, wisdom and resources you need to not quit when life gets tough and it's hard to stay focused. Here are three words that sum up commitment:

SACRIFICE (Set aside your own pleasures and comfort.)

PURPOSE (Find your reason for being here on earth.)

DETERMINATION (Follow through on your decisions until they are complete.)

1. As you consider your involvement with your FFA chapter, another organization or team, which is most difficult for you to live out: sacrifice, purpose or determination?

2. Why must advocates keep clarifying their commitment and refining their message?

_____

_____

3. Is it difficult for you to make long-term commitments? Why?

_____

_____

Self Assessment

Review the five phases of building personal convictions: ideas, opinions, beliefs, commitments, convictions. Now reflect on two decisions you've made recently for a project. The decisions should involve some future plan. Was it difficult to follow through on them? Where do you stand on those two decisions? List these two decisions and circle the stage you think you are in regarding each decision:

Decision:

_____

STAGE: IDEA   OPINION   BELIEF   COMMITMENT   CONVICTION

Decision:

_____

STAGE: IDEA   OPINION   BELIEF   COMMITMENT   CONVICTION

Try It Out

Think about a goal you want to accomplish this year. It could be associated with a project your chapter is working on or a personal goal. You could also choose an idea such as preparing a promotional campaign to launch in your community to raise awareness on a specific issue such as food waste or animal care. Once you select your goal, write out a detailed action plan with target dates for completion. Share it with some of your fellow members and ask them to hold you accountable.

IMAGE TWO
[Facebook or TV]

Facebook or TV

IS YOUR MESSAGE A ONE-WAY TRANSMITTAL OF INFORMATION OR AN INVITATION FOR LISTENERS TO ENTER THE CONVERSATION? THE BEST LEARNING OCCURS IN A SOCIAL CONTEXT. PEOPLE LEARN BEST IN COMMUNITY AND IN RELATIONSHIP WITH THE COMMUNICATOR OR FELLOW LISTENERS. WORLDVIEW EMERGES FROM INTERACTION.

Did you see the movie *The Social Network* when it came out in October of 2010? It was all about how Facebook was launched from a university dorm room by a couple of Harvard students. While Mark Zuckerberg claims there's a bunch of fiction in the story—it remains a testament to one thing: People love to interact. We're social and love to be connected. We love the volley of a conversation, and we love to update others on what's happening in our lives.

Compare Facebook, Twitter and Instagram with television. Do you realize that people spend more time on Facebook and other such sites than they do watching TV? You read that right. We spend more hours on the Internet than we do watching television. This fact has television network executives scrambling to discover ways to draw folks back to TV programs. Their research has turned up these findings:

Social networking sites like Facebook are so effective because:

1. It's about people you know or want to know better.

2. It invites interaction and connectivity with others.

3. It makes communication simple and fast.

4. It allows contact with others to occur in real time.

This explains the failure of so many "canned" television programs. It also explains the presence of more and more "reality" TV shows. It's why shows like *The Voice* and *Dancing With the Stars* allow viewers to vote on who stays on the show. It also illustrates why more and more shows allow people to tweet or text the performers as they watch a program, to be a part of the action.[1] We want to weigh in. We want to have a say in the direction of the program. Let's get honest—some of us want to be the star.

Effective communicators and advocates recognize this. They know that if they're going to get a message across to an audience, they must let the people do some of the talking. In conversation, talking too much doesn't make a favorable impression on listeners. People who talk too much pay a price and lose a certain degree of credibility. Few people want to sit passively and simply listen to someone lecture for an hour. Great speakers know when to "get off the stage." This simply means that when we are communicating, we understand when we've said enough for now, and we pause to allow listeners to respond. Depending on the size of the audience, you can do this a number of ways:

1. Place your audience in small groups of three or four to discuss a well-crafted question such as, "Can you describe a time in your life where the concept we are discussing had an impact on you?" Or "Who do you know that practices this concept well and how do they do it?"

2. Choose a person or two to represent the audience and join you on stage to interact.

3. Allow for a question-and-answer period during your presentation.

4. Provide a way for listeners to tweet or text in comments to the speaker.

5. Create a game or activity for audience members that relates to the topic.

How EPIC Are You?

The fact is, listeners will have less and less mercy for one-way information as time marches further into the twenty-first century. If you're a great communicator, they will put up with it longer than they will for average speakers, but eventually, all audiences want to respond. If they cannot, they realize the time they're spending won't transform them. A mentor once told me:

"There is no life change without life exchange."

I believe this statement from the bottom of my heart. As a rule, people must wrestle with a topic themselves, not merely sit passively and hear about it from someone. The messages that get through are the ones that invite participation from the audience. Dr. Leonard Sweet, a futurist and college professor, was correct when he said this generation is an EPIC Generation:

E – EXPERIENTIAL
They don't want a sage on the stage with a lecture, but an experience.

P – PARTICIPATORY
They want to participate in the outcomes of where a message goes.

I – IMAGE-RICH
They grew up with visual images and prefer them over facts and figures.

C – CONNECTED
They are connected socially and technologically with people.

Whenever any of our Growing Leaders team presents a Habitudes Experience® on a school campus, we never simply teach *Habitudes* verbally. That would miss the point completely. We use eight building blocks during the conference that include slides, music, small-group discussion, videos, personal interviews, games, panel discussion and journal time. Whatever the learning style of each audience member, we will touch on it as we allow people to interact with the topic, the speaker and each other. Everyone participates.

If you've read the book *A Million Miles in a Thousand Years* by Donald Miller, you know the true story of the Goff family in San Diego and their New Year's Day Parade. More than a decade ago, when the kids were young, the family sat around bored on New Year's Day. Dad decided boredom wasn't fitting for a day that God made, so he asked the kids for suggestions, and they decided to have a family parade down their small street. And as they notified neighbors, the family decided NOBODY could watch their parade. Folks must participate. Now the parade is huge. It's an annual street tradition, complete with a Grand Marshal and Queen. And nobody is allowed to watch. Nobody can sit on the curb. Everyone marches in the parade. It's a wonderful story about how much better life is when we participate.[2]

RESEARCH SAYS

Loads of relevant research has been done by educators, such as Dr. Alexander Astin and Dr. Helen Astin from UCLA, Dr. Bill McKeachie from the University of Michigan and Dr. George Kuh at Indiana University, and Dr. Lev Vygotsky from Russia also had done some earlier research on this topic. These scholars provide helpful data on how people—particularly young people—learn best. I've listed three of their discoveries below. I think these are all important to consider in your work as an advocate, especially with your peers:

ACTIVE INVOLVEMENT – Student success increases with the degree or depth of student engagement in the learning process. When we increase the amount of time and energy students must invest in their experience, transformation increases as well.

SOCIAL INTEGRATION – Student success is deepened through human interaction, collaboration and formation of interpersonal relationships among students and members of the community. When we increase interaction in the educational process, learning increases.

SELF-REFLECTION – Student success is strengthened when students reflect on and internalize their learning experiences, transforming these experiences into a form they can apply. When we allow time for listeners to reflect on data, retention increases.

Recently, I spoke at two events on back-to-back evenings. My topic was the same on both nights, so I decided to try a little experiment. On the first night, I provided the best information I possibly could, sharing statistics and stories the audience could relate to and even use. At the end of the night, I could tell people enjoyed it, but something was still missing. Relatively few audience members purchased any books or DVDs at the resource table.

On the following night, I made some changes. After my opening comments, I immediately clustered people in small groups at tables and gave them a question about themselves to answer. They were hooked. In fact, during the next hour, I broke them into groups for discussion and feedback four different times, and I ended the night with a question-and-answer time. The changes I made were simple—but they made a world of difference. People raved about the night, and they bought loads of books and DVDs afterward. They loved it and I think I know why. They got to be the star.

I actually believe that motivation already exists inside of everyone. Great communicators and advocates call people to participate in a topic they value, so they can become the best version of themselves. Case in point: In his book *Drive*, Daniel Pink invites us to imagine it is 1995. Two digital encyclopedias are about to be created. The first is from Microsoft, a stellar company full of smart people and money. It will be sold on CD-ROMs and later online. The second will launch in a few years, driven not by a company but by thousands of ordinary people who write and edit articles for fun. The question is: Which of these two products will survive? No one in their right mind would have predicted the second one—but that's actually what happened. In 2009, Microsoft pulled the plug on Encarta, but Wikipedia continues on as motivated people engage in what they love doing. Participation is everything.

Talk It Over

1. Can you think of times you have seen someone practice this *Habitude* while advocating for agriculture?

_____

_____

2. What role does interaction play in the communication process? How can this type of interaction inspire your listeners to join you as an agriculture advocate?

_____

_____

3. How EPIC is your communication and ability to tell the story of agriculture? Brainstorm a few ways that you could invite interaction from listeners when discussing topics such as urban agriculture.

_____

_____

SELF ASSESSMENT

How interactive is your communication and advocacy? Rate yourself from 1–10, with 1 being the lowest score and 10 being the highest score.

1. I include opportunities for listeners to give feedback.

   < 1   2   3   4   5   6   7   8   9   10 >

2. I invite listeners to interact with one another.

   < 1   2   3   4   5   6   7   8   9   10 >

3. I create opportunities for listeners to reflect and process.

   < 1   2   3   4   5   6   7   8   9   10 >

4. I use a variety of images, videos or illustrations to communicate.

   < 1   2   3   4   5   6   7   8   9   10 >

5. People are more connected as a result of my communication.

   < 1   2   3   4   5   6   7   8   9   10 >

6. When speaking, I gauge the involvement of listeners and adjust accordingly.

   < 1   2   3   4   5   6   7   8   9   10 >

TRY IT OUT

One of the most important roles as a student is to teach others about agricultural topics and engage them in meaningful conversation about these issues. This activity allows you to practice writing a speech using an EPIC grid.

Scenario:

The administration of your school has given you the opportunity to give a speech at Career Day. You will have 15 minutes to share how agriculture impacts our daily lives and the wide array of career opportunities available.

Answer the following questions as you prepare to write your speech:

1. How will students who listen to you get actively involved in the presentation?

_____

_____

2. What images could you use to add a visual component to your speech?

_____

_____

3. Is there a way to leverage social media so the listeners could interact with your speech material?

_____

_____

Once you have written your speech, share it with fellow classmates or a teacher to get input.

Rivers and Floods]

Rivers and Floods

FLOODS AND RIVERS ARE BOTH BODIES OF WATER. FLOODS DAMAGE. RIVERS ARE USEFUL IN MANY WAYS. THE DIFFERENCE? FOCUS. COMMUNICATORS AND ADVOCATES MUST CHANNEL PEOPLE, TIME AND MONEY TOWARD ONE FOCUSED VISION.

I have a picture indelibly etched in my memory. When I was a kid, I remember a horrifying flood sweeping through a town not far from where we lived. I watched the TV intently as reporters showed the expanding body of murky water run through streets, over yards and into houses, restaurants and stores. The rushing water seemed to demolish everything in its path. In my mind, I can still see people standing on the tops of their cars weeping, as they watched their homes collapse and float away—piece by piece.

What started as a simple rainstorm ended up filling the nearby rivers and eventually flowing unmercifully into neighborhoods and strip malls. I remember thinking: How can such a simple thing as water do such damage? Some of my friends took a while to recover from the flood. One of them, in fact, wanted nothing to do with water for over a year. For him, a large body of water without some boundary was a frightening thing.

This is a picture of an important advocacy principle. Many organizations begin very focused, like a river. The leaders possess an idea they want to implement. Soon, however, in their zeal to grow, they begin expanding far beyond the boundaries of their initial vision. If they are good at making widgets, they reason, why not make other products as well? Before long, in the name of meeting needs, generating revenue, or just plain growth—they become a flood instead of a river. They lose all focus and sprawl out in every direction. Like a flood, they end up damaging things. Floods can be shallow, unrestrained, muddy and harmful.

Far too many organizations become floods. Take the computer company IBM for instance. In the beginning, when IBM focused on mainframe computers, the company was very profitable. By the 1980s, however, IBM expanded their product line and barely broke even. In 1991, they were making more products than ever, yet, the company wound up losing $2.8 billion. That's almost $8 million a day!

It's interesting. This rule of advocacy is counter intuitive, working the opposite of what we might think. It seems logical that enlarging product lines would always mean greater profit. It's actually the other way around. Staying focused on your central vision and strength is the key to growth. The airline industry is a good example. "People Express" launched as an airline that focused on no frills, low cost flights. At the first taste of success, they decided to expand beyond that vision. They began to provide first class seats, food, etc. Their profits dropped, and they eventually went out of business.

In contrast, Southwest Airlines entered the industry with a clear, focused vision, similar to People Express. They stuck to their strengths, and for years they've been a rare, profitable company in the airline business. Southwest Airlines refused to diversify; they remained a river. Rivers are much more narrow than floods. They move in one direction. They are a source for both electricity and transportation. Why? Vision and focus. Leaders and advocates must own a focused vision, or the organization will spill-out in too many directions. If the leader isn't focused, the team will chase after every new idea. They will fall prey to every vendor wanting to capitalize on the success. Clear and focused vision harnesses energy. Just watch your team for a while. People lose energy when their direction in life is fuzzy. But they get energized when they catch a clear vision.

Just over fifty years ago, Walt Disney gathered his inner-circle to share his idea of building "Disneyland." It would be known as the "happiest place on earth." Walt's vision was clear and focused. As his team began to get excited about the vision, however, one of the members asked, "Who are you gonna get to build it?" Confidently, Walt responded, "I know exactly who I want to build it. Find me the man who helped put the U.S. Navy back in the Pacific after the bombing of Pearl Harbor. I figure he can do it."

It didn't take long for Walt's team to identify this man. His name was Joe Fowler. Admiral Joe Fowler. Retired Admiral Joe Fowler. When Disney showed up at Fowler's door and challenged him to build a theme park, Joe laughed. "You don't understand. I'm retired. I'm through." Disney quickly realized this guy was going to require some work. Placing pictures on the wall, Walt began to storyboard. After describing in great detail the feel, look, smell, sound and even taste of the park—Joe bought in. He stepped out of retirement and oversaw Disneyland's construction in California.

Twenty years later, the idea of "Disney World" was proposed—and can you guess who was hired to supervise the project? Joe Fowler. This time he was 77 years old. When the Disney team approached him a second time, he sighed again, "You don't understand. I'm retired. I'm through." But as pictures were posted and the vision was cast for their biggest project yet, Joe couldn't help but buy in. He ditched retirement again and oversaw the building of Disney World in Florida.

The story goes on. Ten years later, EPCOT was built in Orlando. Disney once again looked to Joe Fowler to lead the construction. He was now 87 years old.

Joe repeated his objection: "You don't understand. I'm retired. I'm through." But Disney knew Joe was the man. His team communicated the clear, focused vision again. Joe lit up, stepped out of retirement and oversaw the project.

What a picture of the energy that accompanies clear vision. Joe's favorite phrase, "I'm retired. I'm through," was changed to, "You don't have to die 'til you want to." Hmmm. I often wonder how much energy remains bottled up in people because they never learn to focus, or they just plain fail to tap into a clear vision.

Here is the irony of this principle. My friend Mike Kendrick explained it with the following phrase: What you focus on expands. Read that sentence again. Now think about it. If I tell you to focus on finding Toyota Camrys on the road, you will notice these cars everywhere. Why? Because what you focus on expands. So, the goal of a leader is to focus, not expand. Growth is a product of focus. Clarify the vision. Focus your people, time, energy and resources. Remember this: just because you CAN do something doesn't mean you SHOULD. Intensify. Don't diversify.

In order to accomplish this focus, it's important to zero in on a handful of words. In fact, maybe just one word (or concept) that becomes your own. It describes your identity and vision. Some of the best selling products on the market "own" such words. Crest toothpaste owns the word "cavities." FedEx owns the word "overnight." Volvo owns the words "automobile safety." As they focus their energies on a single concept, these companies go deeper and expand in one area. They are like a river, moving in one direction. And being a river is about clear vision and a sharp focus.

TALK IT OVER

1. Many organizations or individuals begin very focused, like a river, but as they expand, they lose their initial vision and become a flood. What are some of the benefits you would have as an agriculture advocate if you had a clear, focused vision?

_____

_____

2. Try to think of some famous people or historical figures that lost their vision. List them below with a brief explanation of how you believe they lost their vision. What was the end result?

_____

_____

Self Assessment

The water in a river represents the people, time, energy and resources you have invested in your organization, team or club. So if you're going to be a river, you have to channel your water well. Consider these questions.

1. How many activities are you trying to perform in your chapter? How about your school or sports team? How thin have you spread yourself? Are you more like a flood or a river?

_____

_____

2. What things should you focus on to be more productive? What things should you trim back on?

_____

_____

Try It Out

Dr. Norman Borlaug is a great model for a visionary agriculture advocate. He won the Nobel Peace Prize in recognition of his lifetime of work around one issue: to prevent hunger and famine around the world through better agricultural production. As you think about his example, write down one or two areas in agriculture that you are most passionate about and have the most interest in. It could be issues such as organic food production, foreign food aid or the use of pesticides. This will help you determine your individual advocacy "river."

Then, during your next class discussion or at your next FFA meeting, ask if you can help to lead a discussion to get your fellow members to describe what agricultural issues they are most passionate about. Tally all of the results and identify one or two areas that your entire chapter would want to focus on for the next year.

From a personal perspective, determine if there is a specific goal you want to accomplish as a student. Do you want to learn more about where your food comes from? Do you want to run for chapter office? Do you want to earn an FFA degree? Do you want to lead efforts to help your chapter win a National Chapter Award?

Write out the specific steps you need to take to achieve the goal.

Are their areas in your life where you need to say "no" in order to stay in the "flow" of your chosen "river?"

IMAGE FOUR

[Number Three Pencil]

Number Three Pencil

A PENCIL COMPANY COULDN'T EVEN GIVE AWAY ITS #3 PENCILS. WHY? THEY ARE TOO HARD TO USE. COMMUNICATORS AND ADVOCATES MAKE THEIR MESSAGE USER-FRIENDLY. THEY KEEP THINGS SIMPLE, NOT HARD. BOTH THE BIG IDEA AND THE ACTION STEP THEY HOPE FOR ARE SIMPLE TO GET AND TO TAKE.

Years ago, a pencil company located next to a university decided to make a donation to the school. The executives wanted to demonstrate good public relations by providing a pencil to every student enrolled at the college. They chose, however, to give the student body #3 pencils, not #2 pencils. They had more of them in stock.

When they gave away the pencils—they discovered the students didn't like them or use them. Within one day, pencils were found in the garbage cans and on the grounds of the campus. No one seemed to want them. When staff members finally asked the students why they didn't use them, the response was unanimous: the pencils were too hard. To use a #3 pencil, you had to push down on the paper so hard, it was not worth it to write with them. Students went back to using other means to take notes.

Herein lies another truth for communicators and advocates. Whatever it is you are attempting to communicate, people won't use it or apply it if it is too hard. If your message becomes complex or too difficult to understand, the average person will mentally check out—even if they were interested in the beginning. Let me give you an example. I have been in countless meetings where announcements were made about upcoming events or where the restrooms are or how to get involved in some activity on campus. For some reason, the presenter begins to get lost in the details: "If you want to sign up for the event next week, just go down the third hallway, and go through the wide door on the left. No, make that the right. Then, just go into the room and look for the green table. There should be a clipboard with some sign-up sheets. If there isn't, look for a sign-up sheet on the yellow table. If you can't find one, just grab a piece of paper and write your name and student ID number and leave it by the desk beside the cabinet. Hope to see you there."

Now—I may be exaggerating a bit—but do you see my point? The message and the action step are so complex, people just give up somewhere in the middle of it. Too confusing. Too many details to remember. They think to themselves: *I don't want to get involved that bad. It's too hard.*

Just like a #3 pencil, people won't use a message if it is too hard.

Great communicators and advocates challenge audiences to achieve difficult goals. The difference is, they simplify their message to be easy to understand, and the initial action step they ask for is simple to take. In other words, great communicators keep it simple.

In *The Social Animal,* David Brooks profiles the lives of a couple, Harold and Erica, to explain some of the most fascinating aspects of human nature. In one scene, he shares an insight Erica learns by attending meetings full of top international leaders: "She often would sit back in the middle of some long meeting and wonder how it was that these men and women had risen to the top of the global elite. They weren't marked by exceptional genius. They did not have extraordinarily deep knowledge or creative opinions. If there was one trait the best of them possessed, it was a talent for simplification. They had the ability to take a complex situation and capture the heart of the matter in simple terms. A second after they located the core fact of any problem, their observation seemed blindingly obvious, but somehow nobody had simplified the issue in quite those terms beforehand. They took reality and made it manageable for busy people."[3]

THE SIR WINSTON METHOD

Winston Churchill was a brilliant communicator. He was the perfect advocate to call England to face Nazi imperialism during World War II. Dozens of times, he'd stand in front of a crowd of citizens or parliament members or in front of a radio microphone and sound the cry to stand with him and refuse to surrender the values of the free world. Churchill had a simple pattern he followed that always seemed to work as he spoke to fearful listeners who were preoccupied with a poor economy and a looming enemy. Here is the "Sir Winston Method:"

1. STRONG BEGINNING – He jumped right into the topic with a key fact, quote, story or statistic.

2. SIMPLE LANGUAGE – He didn't try to impress listeners with big words most would not know.

3. ONE THEME – He stuck to one, central big idea and refused to clutter it with lots of sub-points.

4. PICTURES – He knew that people remembered metaphors or stories, so he gave them one.

5. EMOTIONAL ENDING – He closed by engaging listeners at the heart level and casting vision to act.[4]

Churchill understood the Number Three Pencil truth. Don't make it hard. Keep it simple and clear. Share one big idea. Call for one action. He knew that communicators and advocates are information architects. They must design their ideas to be clear and simple, introducing details only when people have grasped the big picture and are ready for more. Good communicators, in fact, boil their message down to one simple sentence and one clear objective.

Sounds easy, doesn't it? Here's what makes practicing this *Habitude* difficult. When crafting your message, you'll generate lots of new ideas along the way. This can lead to a gradual expansion of your message's goal. It's what some call a "scope creep." The scope of your message has crept out of bounds and now you're tempted to share so many great ideas you've discovered. Sadly, many cloud the issue and sidetrack listeners from the simple idea and goal you had at the start. The best way to combat this is to write down a simple statement of your message as you begin and the one simple objective (action step) you want people to embrace in the end.

It has been said, "If you chase two rabbits, you won't catch either of them." Chip and Dan Heath share a translation of that phrase for communicators: "If you say three things, you don't say anything."[5]

Organizations that practice this principle flourish: Nike, Apple and Disney. Others that don't keep their message simple seem to struggle. Take Yahoo! for example. Their message has been clouded by so many different visions that seemingly are unrelated. None of them are bad—it's just a #3 Pencil. Yahoo! is too hard to define or identify, according to former Yahoo! executive, Tim Mayer. They've lost ground to competitors who have one simple message. In contrast, organizations like TOMS Shoes and Charity: Water have changed the face of charitable giving—through simplicity. TOMS Shoes says: Buy a pair of shoes and we'll donate a pair to a child in a developing nation. Charity: Water says: For $20, you can provide water to one person in Africa.

Malcolm Gladwell wrote about a college that distributed booklets all over campus, encouraging students to get tetanus shots. The booklets detailed why it's so important to get the shot—but alas, a small percentage of students responded. Later, the ineffective booklets were changed. They simply headlined that vaccinations were important and provided the exact location and times to get them. That's it. One big idea and one action step. Interestingly, seven times as many students responded.[6] That's the power of clarity and simplicity. And a case against #3 Pencils.

1. Why is it difficult to practice this *Habitude* when describing complex agricultural issues?

_____

_____

2. There are many readily available sources of information about agriculture. Why is it important for agriculture advocates to simplify their message?

_____

_____

3. Who have you heard from recently that practiced this *Habitude* well? Have you heard others who have violated this practice when speaking about agriculture? What was the outcome in each situation?

_____

_____

4. What is the number one reason you struggle when talking about agriculture with your friends who have no agricultural background?

_____

_____

SELF ASSESSMENT

Take a moment and evaluate your personal habits regarding simplicity. Put an X on the dotted line where it most accurately displays your style, and then explain why you scored yourself this way:

1. When you speak, do you most often try to be simple or complex?

   SIMPLE _ _ _ _ _ _ _ _ _ _ _ _ _ _ _ _ _ _ _ COMPLEX

2. When you speak, are you prone to enlisting action or sharing information?

   ENLIST ACTION _ _ _ _ _ _ _ _ _ _ _ _ _ _ _ _ _ _ _ SHARE INFORMATION

Please note: Although none of the above pursuits are wrong. Practicing the Number Three Pencil *Habitude* increases the effectiveness of your message by making it simple, clear and action-oriented.

TRY IT OUT

With the Sir Winston method discussed within this *Habitude* in mind, imagine you are walking into a restaurant wearing your FFA jacket and someone stops to ask you about FFA and agriculture, as they're curious as to the importance of the agricultural industry.

Is your goal to inform, to encourage, or to persuade? Is it to know something, to feel something, or to act?

1. In one simple sentence, write out what your listeners should know as they walk away.

_____

_____

A. How can you simplify your message? Did you eliminate agricultural specific acronyms and vocabulary?

_____

B. Is your closing engaging and does it make a call to action?

_____

2. Write down a summary of the message you are trying to communicate in the limited time you have to prepare.

_____

_____

A. What will be your strong beginning?

_____

B. How can you use a metaphor, analogy, or story to share your points?

_____

How did this process help you simplify your message?

_____

_____

IMAGE FIVE
[The Faded Flag]

The Faded Flag

TOO MANY MESSAGES NEVER GET THROUGH AND PEOPLE DON'T IMPROVE. INFORMATION WITHOUT APPLICATION MAY BE INTERESTING, BUT IT CAN CLOUD THE SUBJECT. LIKE A FADED FLAG, IT SENDS NO CLEAR MESSAGE. WE MUST RELAY CLEAR INFORMATION AND CHALLENGING APPLICATION IF WE ARE TO CHANGE ANYONE'S MIND.

The story's told of a horrible train wreck that took place in North Carolina long ago. A passenger train continued full steam ahead over a broken bridge, derailed and plunged down a hill, killing everyone on board. Despite the flagman waving a flag, signaling the engineer to stop since the bridge was out, the train forged ahead into the death trap.

A lawsuit was filed soon after, claiming that the flagman had failed to wave the red flag as he was supposed to, warning the train to stop. During the court case, the flagman insisted he did wave the red flag and couldn't understand why the train ignored his signal. A witness claimed he waved a white flag, which communicated all was safe to proceed. Finally, an attorney suggested they retrieve the flag and discover who was right. That's when the truth became clear.

The flagman had been honest. He did indeed wave a red flag. The old flag, however, had been weathered in the sun over the years, fading into an almost-white flag—sending the wrong signal.

This story and *Habitude* are relevant for communicators today. Frequently, I hear communicators and advocates waxing eloquent with their facts and figures, but they fail to lead to any clear application. The audience doesn't know what to do with the message. Afterward, even if people liked the talk or were inspired by it, the words don't result in any outcome. Like the flagman, it doesn't matter how passionately we wave our flag or jump up and down, the message is fuzzy. The desired action steps remain unknown and the audience leaves…unchanged.

This happens far too often to advocates. They forget that the people they're speaking to haven't been thinking about the subject of their speech as much as they have. The end result? The speaker assumes the audience understands more than they do, but in reality the action steps remain unclear. The truth of the Faded Flag complements the truth of the Number Three Pencil. Here is the difference:

The Number Three Pencil answers the question: *How* do you want me to do what you are asking me to do? The Faded Flag answers the question: *What* do you want me to do? More than anything else, audiences need clarity if they are going to act on your message.

Price Tags

What's the price tag of our faded flags? Confusion, inactivity, wrong action and unwanted results. Folks can get inspired, excited, even motivated…but you'll get no action. And it's not the unwillingness of the audience to act; it's the uncertainty and lack of clarity they feel about the action. I believe that people, especially young people, want to improve and I've seen this to be especially true in FFA. You want to get better. In fact, I think you actually yearn for a challenge that will engage you to work at your very best. I've said for years that students hunger to participate in projects that are very important and almost impossible. Sadly, as communicators and advocates, we often dilute our messages to make them more palatable. We become fuzzy or confusing by not speaking with conviction or clarity. We're afraid of rejection. Of complacency.

I love the legendary story of Ernest Shackleton, who led many expeditions to Antarctica in the early twentieth century. He once posted a recruitment flyer with the following statement:

> *Men wanted for a hazardous journey. Small wages. Bitter cold, long months of complete darkness, constant danger; safe return doubtful. Honor and recognition in case of success.*

The stunning part of this story is—more than 5,000 men responded. It's interesting to me that Shackleton didn't push people to join, nor did he persuade them with how fun, easy or beneficial it would be. He simply laid out the clear challenge and gave people a chance to reply. It was attractive in its brutal honesty. No syrup. No glitz. No artificial sweeteners. Just a straightforward pitch: Here is the deal.

I believe that your generation is magnetically attracted to such a pitch. You can smell persuasive gimmicks and pretense a mile away. The reason more don't step out and get involved or take a risk is simple—communicators and advocates fail to be clear, compelling or to call for big action. That's what this *Habitude* is about. People long for:

- Clear information (Here is the pitch.)

- Challenging application (Here is the price.)

Clear Information

In 1990, Elizabeth Newton performed her PhD project at Stanford, called "Tappers and Listeners." Chip and Dan Heath mention it in their book *Made To Stick*. It was a simple exercise where a group of individuals was divided into two teams. The first team was called "tappers," and their job was to choose a song from a list of twenty-five well-known songs (such as "Happy Birthday" or "The Star-Spangled Banner") and tap out the song on a table with their fingers. The second team was the listeners. Their job was to simply guess the song by the rhythm being tapped. Sound simple?

In reality, the listener's job was quite difficult. Of the 120 songs that were tapped out in Newton's experiment, only 3 were guessed correctly. That's 2.5 percent. Not a very good score. Now, here's what made the experiment newsworthy. Before the tappers began, each of them was asked to predict the odds of their listeners getting the song right. The tappers predicted their odds were 50 percent. They thought they would get their message across one time in every two. Interestingly, the tappers only got their message across one time in forty. Why? It's simple. When tappers tap a song out, they're hearing the song in their head. Most listeners didn't hear the song at all, even though they heard the beat. These tappers were stunned at how hard the listeners were working in order to guess the song.[7] Isn't it obvious?

Unfortunately, this little exercise is repeated so many times between communicators and audiences. The one talking assumes the listeners will "get it." It's simple. The fact is, listeners have their minds in so many different places—their biases may cause them to misunderstand the message the communicator is sending. So what can we do?

1. Summarize the "big idea" and make sure everything you say in your outline supports it.

2. Share the idea and the supporting content with a couple of middle school students. If they get it, you can proceed to share it with older audiences.

Challenging Application

Once you nail down the issue of clarity, the important thing is to generate an action step that's robust and compelling. The challenge you give your listeners will make or break your success. In a sense, you're at the tollbooth, and your listeners are all in their respective cars. You then say: "Here's the price of the toll. I'm asking for you to pay it." When pondering the appropriate action, ask yourself:

- What is it we really need to accomplish?
- What will prevent us from achieving it?
- What is the first big step?
- When will they take it?

Assuming the purpose of our communication is changing perception, let me pose this statement: *Information without application is a faded flag.* We must challenge people to change, but we also must let them know the price. Then we need to encourage them to pay it—in order to grow. We must ask for it. People love growing toward a goal when it is significant. If you challenge the status quo, they will hunger to take a journey with you. They have high expectations of anyone "up front" and on stage, so challenge the norm. *Be clear to communicate that change always has a price.*

Talk It Over

1. Think out loud. What is the goal of most of your communication and advocacy:

   A. Persuade

   B. Enlighten

   C. Encourage

2. When communicators and advocates fail to foster lasting life change, what is it that's missing? Do you see any patterns in speakers who are unable to move audiences?

   _____

   _____

3. Why do you suppose it's so important for communicators to offer a big challenge to people?

   _____

   _____

4. Do you have a hard time making the "ask" when you are speaking to a group about important agricultural issues? What makes it difficult?

   _____

   _____

Self Assessment

Rate yourself on how clearly you are able to declare the "price" of change and ask for it. Mark an "X" where your communication lands on the spectrum:

1. I am able to build a strong and clear case for the agricultural subjects I speak about:

   No _ _ _ _ _ _ _ _ _ _ _ _ _Somewhat _ _ _ _ _ _ _ _ _ _ _ _ _ _ _Yes

2. I am able to create and describe an action step for people to take in my communication:

   No _ _ _ _ _ _ _ _ _ _ _ _ _Somewhat _ _ _ _ _ _ _ _ _ _ _ _ _ _ _Yes

3. I am able to ask for a significant response from my listeners:

   No _ _ _ _ _ _ _ _ _ _ _ _ _Somewhat _ _ _ _ _ _ _ _ _ _ _ _ _ _ _Yes

Try It Out

Imagine that some of your state legislators have accepted an invitation to attend your agricultural program or FFA banquet. You have been asked to help host them at the event, and you will sit next to them at the dinner table.

You want to take advantage of this opportunity to talk with these legislators about an important agricultural issue facing your state, and you want to give a young person's perspective to these legislators.

Ask yourself the following questions:

1. What is the biggest agricultural issue my state is facing today?

   _____

   _____

2. What is the clear information I want to convey on the issue?

   _____

   _____

3. What is the desired action step I want the legislator to take?

   _____

   _____

4. What is the most compelling and creative way I can make my message "stick" long after the legislator has left the event?

   _____

   _____

Movies or Meetings

WHICH WOULD YOU RATHER ATTEND: A MEETING OR A MOVIE? ARE YOU
KIDDING? 99% OF THE TIME, PEOPLE WOULD MUCH RATHER GO TO A MOVIE THAN
A MEETING. WHY? MOVIES CONTAIN ELEMENTS THAT MOST MEETINGS DON'T:
STORY. CONFLICT. ACTION. RESOLUTION. GOOD COMMUNICATION CONTAINS
THOSE ELEMENTS AS WELL.

Years ago, I heard author Pat Lencioni speak on teamwork. When he mentioned
the fact that most team members hate going to meetings—all of us agreed. Pat
began searching for why that was the case. It was at that point he began posing a
question to business leaders everywhere:

Given a choice, would you rather go to a meeting or a movie?

You can imagine the responses he received. The vast majority of people naturally
chose a movie, hands down. Not even close. Then, Pat played the devil's advocate.
He bantered by saying, "Why? Movies have nothing directly to do with your
life, while meetings often do; in fact, in meetings you are allowed to speak up
and weigh in on decisions." Why then do people prefer going to a movie over
a meeting?

I believe it's the same reason most people would rather go to a movie than hear
a speech. Very often, speakers are guilty of leaving out the same ingredients that
meetings often neglect. Movies, on the other hand, almost always include them:

- STORY
- CONFLICT
- ACTION
- RESOLUTION

Communicators and advocates can be tempted to feel like telling a story isn't very
scholarly. Further, we tend to avoid disagreement at all costs. After all, we don't
want to create conflict in the audience. This means there is no need for action and
resolution, the very items that attract audiences to movies.

Think about it. The very elements that cause millions of Americans to go to movies each week are the elements so many speakers deliberately leave out of their messages. It's no wonder the words "speech" or "sermon" have negative connotations to them. Both sound boring.

According to author Daniel Pink, we live in an increasingly right-brained world. People relish imagination and story more than they do facts and figures. They want their lives to be a story worth telling, and they want to have a great soundtrack to go along with it. The same is true for the messages they listen to. Hollywood producer Ralph Winter suggests that narrative and storytelling are central to our culture. "That's what gets attention out there. The more we tell honest stories... the more we find stories that make connections."[8]

INVITING CONFLICT

The stuff that makes for a good story is conflict. Think about the timeless legends and fairy tales that Disney has made into movies for years. There is a villain. There is a conflict. There is a hero. There is action. There is resolution. It is the conflict, however, that keeps us watching.

Donald Miller once shared how a friend came to him, grieving that his teenage daughter was dating a guy who got into a lot of trouble. The boyfriend had a lifestyle that didn't reflect any of the family's values and, in fact, was both immoral and illegal. Dad didn't know what to do. Miller simply responded by asking if his friend had considered that his daughter may simply be choosing a better "story" than the one he was creating as a father in his home.

When the man looked puzzled, Miller continued—everyone wants to be part of a story that is interesting and compelling. They want their life to resolve a conflict. This man's daughter had simply decided her life at home was boring—and her boyfriend wasn't.

This suggestion got his friend to re-think his family's story. Over the next few months, the father did some research and found a way to make his family's story more captivating. Over dinner, this father shared about an orphanage in Mexico that desperately needed help. They needed a building, some supplies and some workers from the U.S. to accomplish their goals. He shared his plans to get involved. In a matter of weeks, his kids were intrigued. His son suggested they visit this orphanage in Mexico, and later, his daughter figured out a way to raise money for it online. Over the next year, this family's story was full of conflict and resolution. In fact, it was downright exciting. Eventually, the teenage daughter approached her father and told him she'd broken up with her boyfriend. I think I know why she didn't need the guy anymore. She had found a better story at home.

This is the transformation advocacy efforts must undergo. They need to move from a boring transmission of data to a compelling story that resolves a conflict. Just like a meeting is boring, so are most of our talks.

Meetings are great for sharing information, organizing the efforts of a team and setting goals. But good presentations invite us to join our life story with something even bigger. We find purpose in pursuing more than a task when we participate in a compelling story.

As communicators and agriculture advocates, we must remember that a good story is a compelling part of the communication process. Through it, we are able to join the head to the heart and inspire—action that mere facts cannot achieve.

LET'S COMPARE AND CONTRAST

Examine the two columns below, contrasting movies with meetings.

MEETINGS	MOVIES
1. Data *Sharing facts*	1. Drama *Viewers identify with stories*
2. Words *Discussion about tasks*	2. Action *Activity is tied to a greater purpose*
3. Obstacles *A pain we avoid*	3. Conflict *A challenge we invite*
4. Goals *Measurable summaries*	4. Resolution *Overcoming what seems impossible*

Which of these two columns above describes your messages? In which of the two columns do you prefer to participate? If you chose the "movie" column, you're not alone. "Narrative imagining—story—is the fundamental instrument of thought," writes cognitive scientist Mark Turner in his book *The Literary Mind*. "Rational capacities depend on it. It is our chief means of looking into the future, of predicting, of planning, and of explaining... Most of our experience, our knowledge and our thinking is organized as stories."[9]

ORDER OF IMPACT

After telling stories for over three decades, I have found the impact of stories varies based on history and proximity to the listener. Note the order of impact stories have on listeners, from most to least:

1. PERSONAL – Most effective because the speaker shares from his or her own life.

2. TRUE STORY/CONTEMPORARY – Effective since listeners are acquainted with characters.

3. TRUE STORY/HISTORY – Somewhat effective as listeners may or may not know characters.

4. FICTION – Least effective, as listeners know the story is not real.

The key for communicators and advocates is to know the goal of your message, then choose the story and conflict that will transport an audience to that place. Donald Miller says it this way: "Screenwriters often begin their story with the end in mind. They know their entire movie is heading toward that scene where Frodo throws the ring into the fire. And they write the movie to get him there."[10]

As an advocate, you can use the power of story to connect with your audience. Begin with the end in mind. Invite the listener on the journey. Introduce conflict and use resolution effectively. These principles will move your communication and advocacy from merely transmitting data to weaving a story that others want to engage with.

TALK IT OVER

1. Who taught you how to speak publicly? Was your first speech informative, persuasive, demonstrative, or entertaining? What did you speak about?

_____

_____

2. How are storytelling and advocating related?

_____

_____

3. Why do so many speakers avoid the elements that make speeches engaging? Why is engagement so important when advocating?

_____

_____

4. What steps do you plan to take to make your messages about agriculture more like a movie?

_____

_____

SELF ASSESSMENT

Take a moment and evaluate your personal habits regarding this principle. Are you able to communicate a stirring message? Put an X on the dotted line where it most accurately displays your style and then talk about why you scored yourself this way:

1. When you communicate, do you tend to favor information or imagination?

   Information _ Imagination

2. When you communicate, do you tend to invite conflict or avoid it?

   Invite _ Avoid

3. When you communicate, would others describe listening to you as being in a meeting or going to a movie?

   Meeting _ Movie

Try It Out

Think about a message you would like to share with a group of friends within your class at school, in your community, or with business leaders. For example: The importance of community gardens or volunteerism.

Once you have the topic in mind, write out your message in the context of a movie script:

1. How can you discuss the issue in the form of a story?

   _____

   _____

2. Where are points of conflict or tension?

   _____

   _____

3. What specific action do you want people to take after listening to you?

   _____

   _____

4. What would a positive resolution of the issue look like? How could you verbally paint the picture of that resolution?

   _____

   _____

Share your scripts with a friend or fellow FFA member to get feedback.

IMAGE SEVEN

[House on Fire]

House on Fire

PEOPLE LEARN ON A "NEED TO KNOW" BASIS. DON'T JUST JUMP INTO YOUR TOPIC; TAKE TIME TO EXPLAIN THE RELEVANCE OF IT. WHY SHOULD THEY LISTEN? IF THEIR HOUSE IS ON FIRE—THEY WILL LISTEN. COMMUNICATORS AND ADVOCATES MUST CREATE INCENTIVE FOR PEOPLE TO BELIEVE THEY NEED TO EMBRACE THE TOPIC AT HAND.

My friend Jeff and I enjoy reminiscing about our childhoods. We both had great moms who made growing up very entertaining. There is one phrase he remembers his mom using over and over again. When Jeff claimed he didn't hear his mom ask him to do something, or when he didn't obey a request she made of him, his mom would say: "If I told you the house was on fire, you'd listen and obey me!"

We have smiled over that "mom phrase" many times. It's true, by the way. There are certain bits of information that make it through our filters and cause our ears to tingle and our minds to perk up. Psychologists tell us that humans perceive information to be relevant when it elicits fear, hope or pleasure. When those three items are a part of the message—people tend to tune in. Obviously, we all want to avoid danger or harm, and we all want to receive pleasure or be improved. A message like "Your house is on fire!" naturally qualifies as a topic we need to listen to and heed. In our world today, however, because the average person receives over 250 commercial messages a day, most messages don't get through.[11] In addition, we receive information via texts, phone calls, Twitter, email, LinkedIn, Facebook and other social media outlets. Add to this radio, YouTube and other Internet sites, as well as actual face-to-face conversations, and you have over one thousand messages coming at you every day. (It makes me weary just thinking about it.) The fact is, most of us couldn't possibly process all the messages thrown at us. We'd be overwhelmed and would shut down. So what do we do? We create mental "filters" to screen out any information that seems irrelevant. It's a coping mechanism nearly all of us have developed—like a muscle—and that muscle is pretty strong, too.

This reality makes it challenging to "get through" as a communicator and advocate. Even good speakers get turned off or tuned out. That's why great ones take the first few minutes of their speaking time and light a "house on fire." Not literally, of course, but they take time to cover the "why" before they get to the "what."

Why is this message so important for the audience? Good speakers know they must create incentive for their listeners to stay with them as they talk. They know that people learn on a "need-to-know" basis. When they feel they need to know, they will listen.

Two math teachers performed a little experiment that demonstrated the truth of this *Habitude*. Both instructors taught "Math in Society" to average teens. One of these math teachers taught his high school juniors the subject straight from the textbook. He got right to the "what" and wasted no time explaining the concepts. You can imagine the kind of grades his students made. Only the gifted students did well. The other teacher took a few minutes before every class period and described how important the concept would be to their future; how the students would need it in their everyday lives. Needless to say, this incentive proved valuable. Both student engagement and performance went up, measurably higher than with the first teacher and class. The difference is simple. The first class didn't have any "house on fire" that they could relate to the subject.

In our world, it isn't enough to simply suggest your topic is important. It must be urgent as well. When something is important, people prioritize it. When it is urgent, they rush to act. For most people, motivation is not merely an intellectual exercise. It is emotional. During my years working with John Maxwell, he often would say that people don't change when it is logical. People only change when they:

- Know enough that they're able to.
- Care enough that they want to.
- Hurt enough that they have to.

Sean D'Souza agrees. He says people don't behave the way you think they will:

- They don't fall in love at first sight.
- They don't eat the moment they feel hungry.
- They don't run to the restroom the moment they feel the need.
- They wait and wait and wait. They don't act until there is great urgency.[12]

So, communicators and advocates must not merely inform people that their house is on fire. They must light a fire under them. Speakers must create the same motivation in people that occurs when...

- They're starving.
- They're scared.
- They have to go to the bathroom.
- They're thirsty.
- They're exhausted.

These are motivating realities that cause a sense of urgency inside a person. They're illustrations of how communicators and advocates must light a fire underneath their listeners. Audiences need to feel that it's urgent to listen and act on what the advocate is saying. Otherwise the information will get lost in the filter. This means speakers must warn them of danger if they don't act; cast vision of what could be if they do act; share the benefits of action; and equip them to know how to act.

CREATING A DILEMMA

Let me explain this concept another way. Effective communicators and advocates create a *dilemma* inside their listeners that the speakers will *resolve* within their talk. The dilemma must come first, or audiences have no incentive to listen. Their minds may be in a million other places. But—if the advocate reminds or enlightens them about a problem that MUST be solved—suddenly, people are all ears. Putting the fire out is urgent.

The ancient Chinese used a little analogy to describe how to ignite the will of a person to action. They believed our will is like a cart that's pulled by two horses. The names of those two horses are the mind and the emotions. If you get both of these horses moving together—you get the will. The incentive we must create is both logical and emotional; it is directed at the mind and the heart.

A story is told about an Alabama football game when legendary Coach Bear Bryant was coaching the Crimson Tide. It was late in the game and Alabama was winning. His quarterback was instructed to keep the ball on the ground and run out the clock. Since the defense was expecting this, Bryant's quarterback decided to throw a pass and surprise everyone. When he did, his worst nightmare was realized. He not only threw an interception, he threw it into the hands of the fastest man on the opposing team. Now—it was an impossible chase to run this man down. Or, so it seemed.

Just before he scored, the quarterback actually caught up to him and tackled him. The clock ran out and Alabama went on to win after all. Afterwards, however, the opposing coach questioned Coach Bryant: "How could your quarterback catch my defensive back? He's faster than anyone on the field!"

Bryant's answer was classic. He smiled and replied, "It's simple. Your man was running for six points. My man was running for his life."

As communicators, we cannot underestimate the role that motivation plays in the lives of our listeners. When we can communicate incentives and create a sense of urgency, action is sure to follow. It's amazing how fast people will act when a house is on fire.

Talk It Over

1. In our day of unprecedented opportunity, why do you believe so many people need us to light a fire underneath them or "set their house on fire" to get them motivated to act?

_____

_____

2. Why do you think people have an urgent need today to know more about agriculture?

_____

_____

3. Can you name some times in your past when a classmate or other leader provided motivation for you to act by setting your house on fire? What did they say about the issue that made you feel compelled to act?

_____

_____

4. As an agriculture advocate, how could you put this _Habitude_ to use right away?

_____

_____

Self Assessment

How well do you provide incentive before you provide information to people? Do you create a sense of urgency? Using the scale from 1–10, with 1 being the lowest score and 10 being the highest, evaluate yourself below:

1. I think about who is listening and I speak to their perspective.

< 1 2 3 4 5 6 7 8 9 10 >

2. I always provide the "why" before I get to the "what" when I speak.

< 1 2 3 4 5 6 7 8 9 10 >

3. I recognize the best way to motivate people and it usually works.

< 1 2 3 4 5 6 7 8 9 10 >

4. People generally listen to me and do what I request that they do.

‹ 1   2   3   4   5   6   7   8   9   10 ›

5. I help listeners clarify the most important response when I speak.

‹ 1   2   3   4   5   6   7   8   9   10 ›

TRY IT OUT

You have been asked to speak in front of an elementary or middle school class and explain why every student should take at least one agricultural education class prior to graduation—even if they don't plan to pursue a career in agriculture. Think about these questions as you craft the best approach:

1. What are the objections they might have to acting on your message?

_____

_____

2. What are the biggest incentives they might have to acting on your message?

_____

_____

3. What are the toughest hurdles they must jump in order to act on your message?

_____

_____

4. What are the initial steps you want them to take in response to your message?

_____

_____

Next, lay out the best approach to "lighting the house on fire" and outline the "why" behind your message before you outline the "what."

Practice your message in front of your fellow classmates or FFA members and then discuss your effectiveness.

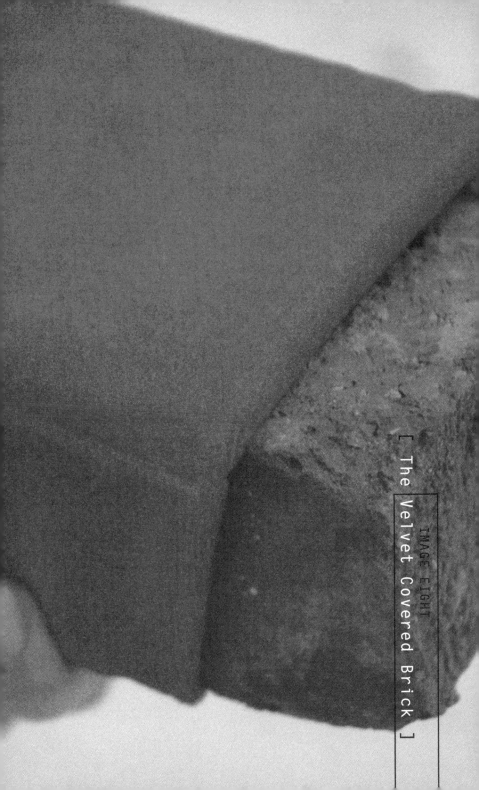

[The Velvet Covered Brick]

The Velvet Covered Brick

GOOD COMMUNICATORS AND ADVOCATES POSSESS BOTH STRENGTH AND SENSITIVITY. THEY ARE TOUGH AND TENDER. THEY ARE SOFT ON THE OUTSIDE (RELATIONAL), BUT FIRM AS A BRICK ON THE INSIDE (PRINCIPLE-CENTERED). BECAUSE THEY ARE EMOTIONALLY SECURE, THEY'RE ABLE TO HANDLE CONFRONTATION AND CONFLICT IN A HEALTHY WAY.

Chip Bell, author of *Magnetic Service: Secrets for Creating Passionately Devoted Customers*,[13] talks about attending a large corporate meeting where the chief executive officer (CEO) stood in front of hundreds of his managers and reported his company's financial history and projected goals. It was strong, well-scripted, and gave clear direction for the future. The scene was a carbon-copy of big-deal annual meetings held in hundreds of ballrooms around the world. But then—something happened that took the meeting into new territory.

Without warning, the CEO moved beyond the teleprompter to the edge of the stage. The speech changed from one of pragmatism to one of passion. When he began to talk about the value of their vision and the power of every team member, he had to choke back tears. Overflowing emotion necessitated several long pauses for him to regain his composure. He bared his soul as he spoke of specific people who had made a difference on the team. As he finished, there was a long silence. The audience sat overwhelmed by what they had just witnessed. Then they leapt to their feet for an awkwardly long standing ovation. Even the tech guys at the sound board were on their feet clapping. This was one different speech.

Bell remembers it wasn't just the CEO's tears that moved his audience. It was his courage to be unabashedly authentic, to be publicly real. Leaders too often associate their mantle of authority with a requirement for detachment. This leader broke the mold. I believe people today long for leaders who are both strong and sensitive. We're complete when our strength leads to sensitivity.

Over the years, I have served as a leader in a for-profit company, three not-for-profit organizations, and two local churches. In every context, I've observed the innate human need people have for leadership and communication that's both tough and tender:

- *In Confrontation*—I needed to be forthright and yet encouraging.

- *In Vision-casting*—I needed to be clear and rational, yet possess character and passion.

- *In Equipping*—I needed to be practical, yet genuine and humane.

- *In Priorities*—I needed to be disciplined, yet flexible.

- *In Managing Relationships*—I needed to be principled, yet warm.

When it comes to dealing with people, the velvet covered brick approach is essential. It's easy to be one or the other—the velvet or the brick. This results in poor or weak communication. Recently, at one company in Washington, the employees met in a conference room during a difficult season. There, the managers abruptly read aloud the names of forty people they planned to fire. They made this announcement the day before the December holiday party. Ugh. At Fob, Inc. in Chicago, employees in a staff meeting were told to go to their desks and check their e-mail. Three dozen of them were sent e-mails telling them that they had been dismissed.[14] Ouch. I heard about one retailer who was confronted by a team member about Barb, a destructive staff person who was violating company policy and values. In fact, she was causing division on the team. The manager just smiled and said, "Oh, that's just Barb. I don't have time to deal with petty issues like that." Slowly, team members began to resign because of Barb. Interesting. What makes a leader mishandle tough situations like these? They don't have the backbone to do it right.

Think for a moment about the great leaders you've observed during your lifetime. The ones we most respect are generally velvet covered bricks. They have a tough and tender side. We saw this in Mayor Rudy Giuliani after the September 11, 2001 attacks on New York City. He was tough and clear as a commander in his direction to city workers, but he was as tender as a chaplain when he attended the funeral services of citizens from the city. We saw it in Herb Kelleher, former CEO at Southwest Airlines, who was a stickler about the values of that airline, but displayed warmth and a sense of humor with his employees. President Ronald Reagan displayed some velvet covered brick qualities as he handled the Cold War and U.S. economic woes with firm convictions in the 1980's, yet he had charisma in front of people who questioned his policies.

COMPARE AND CONTRAST

Let's take a moment to further define what we mean by the "velvet covered brick."

Following are two columns that illustrate the paradoxical qualities leaders and advocates must have:

The Brick	The Velvet
Tough	*Tender*
Doing right	*Being real*
Confronts destructive problems	*Considers diverse perspectives*
Demonstrates strength and courage	*Demonstrates sensitivity and care*
A stickler for results	*A stickler for relationships*
Is strong	*Is susceptible*
Extremely professional	*Extremely personal*
Secure enough to take criticism	*Secure enough to serve your critics*
Possesses convictions about principles	*Possesses compassion for people*
Always embraces the responsibility	*Rarely enforces the rank of the position*

When do we most appreciate a velvet covered brick? During times of conflict. Leaders and advocates who can remain balanced, poised, and maintain a good perspective can handle things better when relationships go sour. In 1983, I began working for Dr. John C. Maxwell. He modeled this principle well. As a new pastor in Lancaster, Ohio, he met a stubborn man named Jim, who was a member of his church. Jim had been responsible for running off the last two pastors at this church. His attitude stunk and his influence was consistently negative. John asked to meet with Jim, and when he did, John got acquainted with him, thanked him for meeting with him—then proceeded to engage Jim about his behavior. Basically, John said to him, "Jim, I have heard from some of our members that you haven't gotten along with the last two pastors here at this church. I also know that you've been influential at this church for many years. Now, the way I see it—you and I could fight over who gets his own way for the next several years; we could make it hell for each other here at this church. Or, we could work together. Jim—I'd like to propose we work together. By that, I mean I'd like to take you to lunch every Tuesday and talk over every major decision with you. You're smart and have influence here. I would welcome your being a part of the direction of this church. Together, I think we could see our greatest days ahead."

John paused, and went on. "Jim—you are 65 years old and it seems to me you have a choice ahead of you. Let's imagine for a moment you decide to work with me, and you have ten more years of helpful service. You could die knowing the ten best years of your life were spent helping a young pastor who desperately needed what you have to offer. Or, you could fight me at every turn, die, and know that your last ten years were spent in a bitter battle with a young man trying to lead this church. Jim, I hope you'll help me. I need you."

At that point, Jim stood up and walked out the door. John Maxwell wasn't sure where he was going or what weapon he may be retrieving…so he followed him out. Jim was hunched over the drinking fountain for what seemed like an eternity. When he stood up and turned around, John realized what was going on inside of Jim. His face was red and bathed in tears. He grabbed John and not only hugged him, he picked him up and said, "Pastor—from now on, I'm in your corner."

Following that day, Jim was a changed man. He was alert and served alongside every decision made in that church. Interestingly, he lived another ten years and died at 75 years old. His wife approached John Maxwell after the funeral, weeping. She said, "Pastor John, the last thing Jim said to me was, 'These last ten years serving in this church were the best years of my life.'"

CONFRONTATION 101

What made those years so good for Jim? A young twenty-something leader who was a velvet covered brick. He was strong enough to confront a tough situation, but sensitive enough to do it with diplomacy and out of genuine relationship. When facing conflict or when someone has done wrong, here are some basic steps I use to confront the people involved:

A. WAIT UNTIL YOUR INITIAL ANGER SUBSIDES.
(Postpone any confrontation until you can be objective.)

B. INITIATE THE CONTACT.
(Don't blame them and wait for them to make things right.)

C. AFFIRM THEM AS YOU BEGIN.
(Thank them for meeting with you and affirm what you can.)

D. TELL THEM YOU ARE STRUGGLING WITH A PROBLEM.
(Own it; it's your problem, not just theirs.)

E. OUTLINE THE PROBLEM; ADMIT YOU DON'T UNDERSTAND.
(Clarify; give them the benefit of the doubt.)

F. SHARE THE PRINCIPLE THAT IS AT STAKE.
(Compromise on opinions but don't violate principles.)

G. ENCOURAGE THEM TO RESPOND.
(Listen well; take notes and understand their perspective.)

H. ESTABLISH FORGIVENESS AND REPENTANCE, IF NECESSARY.
(Create a game plan for change.)

I. AFFIRM YOUR LOVE AND RESPECT FOR THEM.
(End with words of encouragement and friendship.)

The process of confrontation requires emotional security. In 1860, Abraham Lincoln won the Republican nomination over three more highly qualified candidates. Each had more experience, and were household names in the U.S. These rivals were shocked to lose to this backwoods lawyer. Lincoln, however, stunned everyone when he turned around and invited all three to serve on his cabinet. It was a dangerous move, but he later said, "We needed the strongest men in the Cabinet. We needed to hold our own people together. I had looked the party over and concluded that these were the very strongest men. Then I had no right to deprive the country of their service."[15] Now that's a velvet covered brick.

TALK IT OVER

Great leaders and advocates have both a tough and tender side; they are strong yet sensitive. I call it the velvet covered brick approach to communication and advocacy. Today's leaders and advocates need to be relational with people—soft like velvet on the outside. But they also need to hold fast to their principles—firm like a brick on the inside.

1. Think about some great leaders you've observed in the agriculture industry who have adopted the velvet covered brick style of advocacy. It could be a state FFA officer, teacher, or your coach. Describe a time when they balanced the contradiction of being both tough and tender.

_____

_____

2. In contrast, what pitfalls have you observed in leaders who fail to embrace the velvet covered brick style of advocacy?

_____

_____

3. From the "Confrontation 101" section of this *Habitude*, list three steps that are the most difficult for you to put into practice.

_____

_____

SELF ASSESSMENT

Often, leaders and advocates are either too tough or too tender. Which are you? Corporate psychologists have labeled leadership responses to conflict with animal names. Find the one you most identify with:

SHARKS (I really like to get my own way; I win and you may lose, but it's better this way.)

FOXES (We have to compromise; everyone wins a little and loses a little.)

TURTLES (I don't like conflict and I tend to withdraw and not face it.)

TEDDY BEARS (I'll make peace however I can; I don't mind losing so you can win.)

OWLS (Let's work at this and find a way in which everyone can win.)

When you think about how you work as a leader and agriculture advocate, give some examples of why you chose the animal you did.

_____

_____

TRY IT OUT

Think about the people in your chapter with whom you don't always agree or get along with, and consider some of the tough experiences you have shared. As you think about working together as a team of advocates in your school or community, answer these questions:

1. What have your interactions with these people been like in the past? Where are the points of tension?

_____

_____

2. Has this ever impacted the effectiveness of your team when advocating for agricultural issues?

_____

_____

3. What can you do to build your relationships with these peers?

_____

_____

Write down three steps you can take this week to grow these relationships. Share the interactions with your teacher to keep you accountable, so you can become a more influential tough and tender advocate and leader in your chapter.

The Indian Talking Stick

THE INDIAN TALKING STICK REMINDS US THAT BEFORE WE COMMUNICATE AND
ADVOCATE, WE MUST LISTEN. EFFECTIVE COMMUNICATORS AND ADVOCATES SEEK
TO UNDERSTAND THE PERSPECTIVES OF OTHERS BEFORE THEY COMMUNICATE
THEIR OWN POINTS. THEY SHOW EMPATHY AND ASK GOOD QUESTIONS. AS A
RESULT, THEY EARN THE RIGHT TO BE HEARD.

The atmosphere is tense. Conflict is in the air. The two tribes have been known
to disagree before, but recent events have led many to believe that war is on the
horizon. As the council members assemble, the two chiefs join the circle, both
facing each other without saying a word. For several moments there is only
silence…then, in a burst of emotion, the group erupts with angry shouts and
accusations. No one is listening, and it looks like violence is inevitable. That is,
until the visiting chief steps forward and raises the Talking Stick. Suddenly, the
atmosphere begins to change…

It's been around for centuries, yet few have ever heard of it. Here's how it works.
During the meeting, the Indian Talking Stick is passed around from person
to person, but only the one holding it is allowed to speak. It remains in the
speaker's possession until he or she feels completely understood by everyone
in the group. The only exception is when the speaker might lend it to someone
who is seeking to clarify the speaker's point. Once the point is clarified, the stick
returns to the speaker until he believes he is fully understood. Only then is it
passed to the next individual.

It's a simple concept, but the end result is quite remarkable. As the tribal members
pass the stick around, they slowly become less combative and more cohesive. Each
person feels like his or her view is getting a fair hearing. Before long, the real
source of the conflict is revealed, and new solutions are formed. War is averted.
Relationships are restored. All because the focus is on understanding, not just
being understood.

Without question, the greatest emotional need of people today is the need to be understood. And to understand, we must listen. Communicators and advocates *have* to get this. If they don't, it doesn't matter how intelligent, gifted, or charismatic they are. They will ultimately fail to connect with others and end up sabotaging their true potential.

But it's not easy; most of us aren't naturally good at listening (myself included). We have to work at it, being diligent and alert to the needs around us. Case in point: did you know that when the Titanic was sinking, a ship was just thirty miles away that could have come to the rescue? Unfortunately, it never heard the distress call. The radio operator on board had just gone to bed. If he had only listened a little while longer, he would have heard the SOS and turned the ship around. Instead, his ship continued on its way, oblivious to the tragedy unfolding around it.

When it comes to listening, leaders simply cannot afford to fall asleep on the job. Often, as much as 50 percent of leadership is about listening, observing, and interpreting what we see and hear. So how do we learn to do this well? How do we practice the Indian Talking Stick in our everyday lives?

POOR LISTENING HABITS

To start with, we've got to identify the poor listening habits we may have picked up over the years:

• **JUDGMENTAL LISTENING** – jumping to conclusions about the speaker.

• **SELECTIVE LISTENING** – only hearing what you want to hear.

• **IMPATIENT LISTENING** – finishing other people's sentences, interrupting them.

• **EGOCENTRIC LISTENING** – thinking about what you'll say as others are talking.

• **PATRONIZING LISTENING** – pretending to listen, but you're really off in your own world.

• **STUBBORN LISTENING** – listening, but not open—your mind is already made up.

Can you relate to any of these common pitfalls? Your ability to move past them will have a profound impact on your leadership…and your daily interactions with others.

Many leaders and advocates never learn to listen well. They're so focused on their own agendas that they tune out everyone else. The results can be tragic. Robert McNamara confirms this in his book *In Retrospect*.[16] As the U.S. entered the Vietnam War, numerous CIA agents warned top White House officials that failure was inevitable. All the data indicated that the North Vietnamese were a new type of enemy and that a conventional bombing campaign would not work. But their warnings were ignored. By the time the war was over, more than 58,000 U.S. soldiers were either dead or missing in action and little military progress had been made. All because a group of leaders failed to listen.

LEARNING TO LISTEN

If you want to become a great listener and advocate, you need to work on two things: show empathy and ask good questions. Allow me to explain.

SHOW EMPATHY

Empathy is about entering into another person's situation. It involves understanding how others feel and showing that you genuinely care. Counselors are usually great at this. You'll see them nod, show concern in their faces, give an occasional "hmmm," and display real interest in what you're saying. When they listen, you feel understood and your emotions are validated. And here's the kicker: when they finally do speak up, you're all ears. Why? Their ability to listen has earned them the right to be heard. It's the same with us. When we listen empathetically to others, they tend to become receptive to what we have to say in return. They see that we're not focused on advancing our agenda or "winning" the conversation.

I recently met a missionary who worked in Africa for two years without seeing any results. Despite the fact that he was well trained and had earned three doctorates, he couldn't seem to connect with the people there. Week after week his church remained empty. When his son died tragically, he found a local man to help him with the burial. Overwhelmed by grief, the missionary slumped over the casket and began to weep. He sobbed for several minutes. Watching intently, the African man grabbed his hair, picked up his head, and looked him in the eyes. Then, he gently set the missionary's head back down on the pine box, and ran back to the village. He told everyone, "The white man cries like we do." The next Sunday the missionary's church was full.

Why? The people didn't just want a man who impressed them. They were interested in a leader who identified with them. Others want to see that you're human, not a walking encyclopedia. It's an old cliché, but it's true: "People don't care how much you know until they know how much you care." Do the people you lead know how much you care about them? Do they share openly with you?

ASK GOOD QUESTIONS

Showing empathy is important, but so is asking relevant questions. Stop for a second and recall the last time you visited the doctor's office. Did the doctor just barge through the door and immediately begin trying to sell you the latest and greatest drug on the market? I sure hope not! Any doctor worth his or her salt knows that you never give a prescription without first making a diagnosis. Doctors take the time to look into your eyes, listen to your heartbeat, ask where it hurts, etc. Only after poking and prodding will they draw a conclusion and give you a prescription.

Let me ask you a question. Have you learned to poke and prod during your conversations with others? Or, do you make assumptions and jump to conclusions? How you answer says a lot about your listening ability.

Many communicators and advocates are guilty of jamming stuff down people's throats because they believe they're supposed to have answers, not questions. They never ask, afraid they'll appear weak. But asking good questions doesn't make you weak; well-placed questions help you connect with people and understand where they're really coming from. It's a sign of strength.

Making Deposits and Withdrawals

Over the years I've come to realize that great listening is a little like banking. You have to make deposits before you can make withdrawals. It would be silly to walk up to a bank teller and request money if you had never started an account and put money in it! It's the same way with people. We've got to make relational deposits into others' lives before they'll listen to us.

I remember this truth through a little acronym, SALT:

* S – Say anything

* A – Ask questions

* L – Listen well

* T – Turn the topic in a positive direction

I recently had a conversation with a college student. He was getting ready to graduate with a marketing degree and was having doubts on whether or not he had made the right choice. He felt pressure from his parents to quickly find a job right after graduation, so he could start making payments on his student loans. Even though he had made good grades and had served in a significant leadership role on his campus, he admitted to me that he really felt like a failure. I gently said, "I'm so sorry you are going through this tough time. I can only imagine the stress you are feeling right now. Even though I'm not in your same situation, I do have a listening ear, and if you want to talk to someone about it, I'll be glad to listen." The Indian Talking Stick reminds leaders and advocates that if they want to connect with others, they must first learn how to listen. This *Habitude* can revolutionize your day-to-day life. Your relationships will be strengthened and your influence will increase. It all begins with showing empathy and asking good questions. Practice these two and you'll be on your way to connecting with others.

Talk It Over

There is a progression that takes place before a leader and advocate earns the right to be heard. First, we must learn how to listen. Communicators and advocates must focus on understanding others' viewpoints before they can expect to be understood.

1. Why do you think people are more inclined to talk than to listen? As an agriculture advocate, why is it important to maintain good listening skills even when we disagree with someone?

_____

_____

2. Agricultural advocacy occurs on many different platforms—including one-on-one conversations, public speeches, and social media posts. How could you act as a good listener in each of these situations?

_____

_____

3. We sometimes come across members of the general public who show little concern for agriculture, assuming the industry simply doesn't apply to them. Thinking back to the "Indian Talking Stick" strategies, how would you persuade those unconcerned folks to take greater interest in agriculture?

_____

_____

4. Imagine you are walking around the grocery store when a protester approaches you, suggesting you sign a petition to shut down farms in your county. Using the SALT acronym, how would you turn this into an opportunity to respectfully communicate and advocate for agriculture?

_____

_____

5. Asking questions is sometimes associated with appearing weak, but the "Indian Talking Stick" suggests otherwise. Within agriculture, how does asking questions actually strengthen your ability to advocate?

_____

_____

SELF ASSESSMENT

Think about your own listening ability when discussing issues as a communicator and advocate. On a scale of one to ten, how would you rate yourself as a listener?

If you're really brave, have a friend fill it out for you!

1. I display empathy and show genuine interest in others.

   < 1   2   3   4   5   6   7   8   9   10 >

2. My body language shows attentiveness.

   < 1   2   3   4   5   6   7   8   9   10 >

3. I seek to understand before being understood.

   < 1   2   3   4   5   6   7   8   9   10 >

4. I ask relevant questions and engage in others' thoughts.

   < 1   2   3   4   5   6   7   8   9   10 >

5. I am open; I avoid judging others or interrupting them.

   < 1   2   3   4   5   6   7   8   9   10 >

TRY IT OUT

Ryan Bivens started his farming career in 2001 at the age of 22. He and his young wife settled in Kentucky and wanted to farm in a county where neither of them had family or community connections. Money was also tight as they worked to start their business.

Today, Fresh Start Farms has 5400 acres of crops with 68 landlords. And the business continues to expand annually. When Ryan is asked how he has had so much success, he attributes it to relationships. He had to listen and talk with landowners, lenders, managers of government programs, and community members. He also made a point of listening to older farmers to gain from their perspective.

Pair up with another student and write out a communication plan you would implement if the two of you moved to a new town to start a business.

- Who would you want to meet in the town?

- What questions would you want to ask?

- How would practicing the *Habitude* Indian Talking Stick help you be successful?

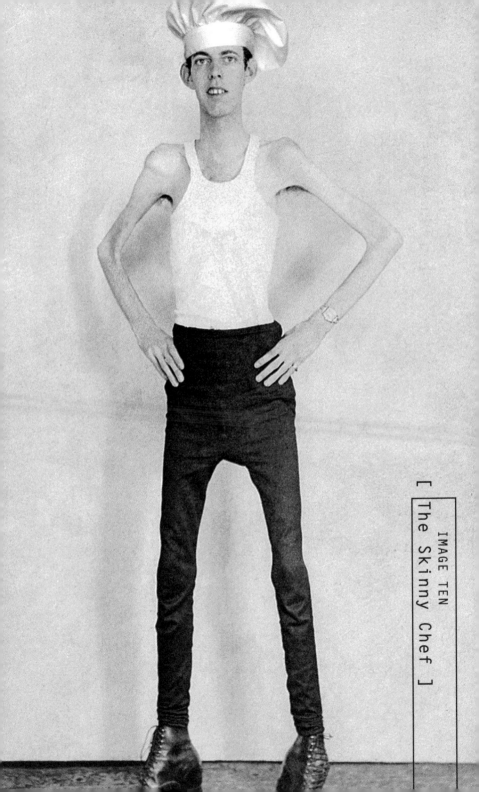

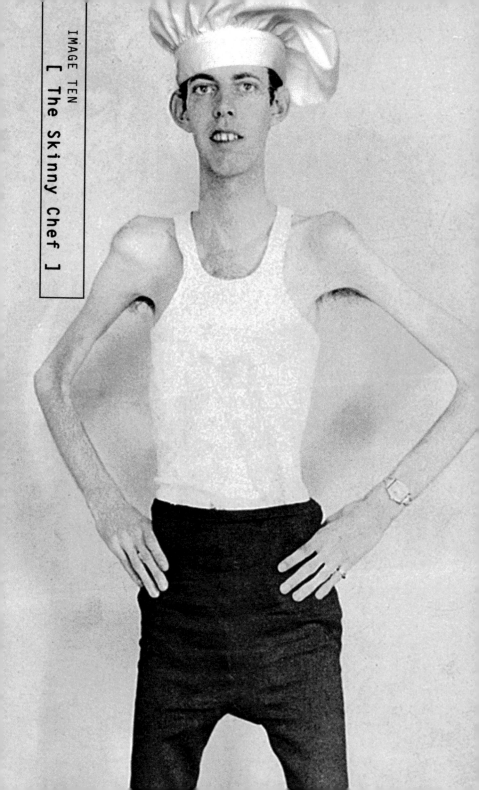

The Skinny Chef

WHO WANTS TO GO TO A RESTAURANT EXPECTING GREAT FOOD—RUN BY A SKINNY CHEF? WHERE'S THE CREDIBILITY? IF THE FOOD'S SO GOOD, WHY DOESN'T HE EAT IT HIMSELF? WHO WANTS TO BUY A CAR FROM A GUY WHO DOESN'T EVEN HAVE A DRIVER'S LICENSE? CREDIBILITY IS ESSENTIAL FOR YOUR MESSAGE TO GET THROUGH.

Imagine you walk into a diner, hoping to enjoy a nice lunch. It's noon and you're hungry. You notice, however, that there are plenty of parking spots outside; there are lots of empty tables and booths inside the restaurant, and several waiters are available to take care of you, as you sit down. Immediately, you begin wondering: why aren't there more people here? It's time for folks to eat. Where are the customers?

Suddenly, everything becomes clear to you. You notice the chef behind the counter. He stands out because he is visibly thin. He is so skinny; it appears like he's not eaten in weeks. Since you're the only customer in the diner, you decide to ask him a question: "How can you be a cook and still remain so thin?"

The chef replies, "Oh it's easy. I never eat anything I cook. I just serve it to the customers."

All at once, you begin to have misgivings about eating lunch at this diner. Why would anyone eat food prepared by someone who never eats it himself? For that matter, why would you purchase a car from a dealer who doesn't even own a driver's license? Or take piano lessons from a teacher who's only read a book about music, but never played the piano herself? It just doesn't make sense. There is no credibility. In fact, this kind of chef, car dealer or piano teacher may just qualify as a hypocrite. All talk and no walk. Their words don't match their life.

George Washington Carver, a famous botanist and scientist, is known today as the inventor of peanut butter. While it isn't true that he invented peanut butter as we know it today, it is said that he devised over 100 uses for the peanut plant including oils, vaccinations and many different foods. What made him so successful, however, wasn't his inventions, but how he used them. George Washington Carver created friendships with some of the most well known people of his time with his kind demeanor and constant willingness to help others.

It is said that Ghandi, Henry Ford, and even Thomas Edison sought him out for his work, but he has almost no patents to his name. Why? "I don't want any discoveries to benefit specific favored persons." He said, "I think they should be available to all peoples." Carver's inventiveness earned him recognition, but his credibility brought him renown.

Perhaps the most important element of effective communication and advocacy is credibility. More than eloquence or great transitions or interesting stories, a speaker must model what they talk about. If an audience doesn't believe the speaker actually knows what they're talking about, or if they sense the speaker doesn't embody what they're demanding of their listeners, they lose all trust. Just like advocacy, effective communication operates on the basis of trust. When advocates must speak on a topic in which they have no experience, they should be honest about it. It's best to admit it up front and even poke fun at the issue. In fact, I've found it's often appealing to tell a story about how I failed to practice the topic. I immediately gain trust through my transparency. Everyone knows I'm not pretending to be someone I'm not.

TRUTH OR FICTION?

I love the old story of the British actor, William Macready. A well-known clergyman once asked him to explain how he drew huge crowds each night in the theater during his stage plays, while the preacher spoke to much smaller crowds in the local churches. The preacher couldn't understand, since Macready's words were only fiction on a script, while he was speaking about eternal issues that could actually determine to their future. Macready's response was insightful. He said, "The answer to your question is simple. I present my fiction as though it were true. You present your truth as though it were fiction."

Ouch. I wonder if that could be said of most speakers. Actors are often much more believable than speakers on a stage. Frequently, we are not real. We are not believable.

This idea is particularly paramount today. In our culture, full of social media profiles, photos and tweets that spin our story exactly as we want others to hear it, appearances have become everything. Many people are far more concerned with how they appear to be than who they really are. Image is more important than integrity. We all know how to look good. We learn quickly how to erect facades in our lives. Maybe this is why authenticity and transparency are so appealing. It's so refreshing when someone opens their mouth and speaks words that are honest, forthright and original. It is magnetic when a communicator speaks and it is clear they actually live the life they challenge their audience to live. They do it before they tell others to do it.

For years, I have worked with college students who would start a band out of their garage. Often, they'd ask me how to best promote their band or their speaking skills or their latest concert tour. (Each of them wanted to make it big time.) Should they print up business cards, launch a website, start tweeting, begin blogging or what? My advice is almost always the same. I tell them to go do what they do locally before taking their act on the road. In other words, before you worry about becoming famous, just execute your gift right at home, perhaps in front of a small crowd or at a low-paying event. Model the way first. Gain credibility by setting an example. Then you'll have stories to tell and credibility to sustain you…and you'll have others do your promoting for you.

My rule of thumb is simple. Each time I'm communicating to audiences, I have found it's helpful to share two examples of how I have interacted with the big idea. It may be a success or a failure, but by illustrating from my personal life, I am able to demonstrate credibility.

During the nineteenth century, Father Damian moved to Molokai, Hawaii, to work in a remote colony among lepers. He was a Catholic priest who had a passion for helping those stricken with leprosy to build skills and learn how to manage their disease. Each Sunday, he would gather them in a church and speak the words, "You lepers must remember that God loves you."

They were nice words, but spoken by a healthy man who couldn't really understand what it was like to have leprosy. Villagers appreciated Father Damian, but his words were theory. Then it happened. After sixteen years of caring for the emotional, physical and spiritual needs of the community, he stood up one Sunday and said something slightly different: "We lepers must remember than that God loves us." He had everyone's attention. It was during the previous week that Father Damien had contracted leprosy himself, by working so closely with the people. He eventually died from it years later, but only after making a huge impact on the colony. He was one of them. That's credibility.

Just like no one wants to eat food prepared by a chef who doesn't eat it himself, no one wants to hear a speaker who doesn't practice the words he speaks. Prime Minister Winston Churchill believed an audience can be *convinced* only when they see you care about *them* and about *what you are talking about.* Churchill learned this from an American politician and mentor named Bourke Cockran. "He was the only one ever to keynote three national political conventions. Churchill once asked Cockran, 'Bourke, what is the secret of eloquence?' Cockran summed it up in one word: 'sincerity.'"[17]

Talk It Over

1. Based on your experience, do you agree that we more easily believe the message of someone who has credibility and experience? Why or why not?

_____

_____

2. Have you ever noticed communicators and advocates trying to spread a message they didn't truly practice? What signs did you see that told you this was likely the case?

_____

_____

3. What are some steps you can take to make the agricultural messages you're trying to communicate become more credible to your audiences?

_____

_____

Self Assessment

Provide a short answer to each of the personal questions below:

1. What leads you to believe that you are credible?

_____

_____

2. Identify three agricultural topics in which you are confident in your credibility.

_____

_____

3. In which topics do you need to develop credibility concerning the subject you're advocating?

_____

_____

4. List a few steps you could take to increase credibility in the areas you listed above.

_____

_____

Try It Out

Imagine that you are preparing to interview for a summer job. You have studied the job description and see that in some ways you are very qualified for the position, but you are lacking experience in other areas. Think through ways to put this *Habitude* into practice before you complete the application and go to the in-person interview.

1. How will you share your successes and positive work experiences?

_____

_____

2. How will you transparently discuss areas where you lack experience, but still have the work ethic and attitude to learn quickly?

_____

_____

3. How can you demonstrate credibility to a future employer?

_____

_____

School Yearbook

WHAT'S THE FIRST PHOTO YOU LOOK FOR WHEN YOU GET YOUR SCHOOL YEARBOOK? IT'S YOUR OWN. WE ALL WANT TO SEE WHERE WE FIT INTO THE STORY. THE SAME IS TRUE WITH LISTENERS. COMMUNICATORS AND ADVOCATES MUST KNOW THAT PEOPLE ARE ASKING: WHERE DO I FIT IN? WHAT'S RELEVANT TO ME IN THIS MESSAGE? WHAT'S IN IT FOR ME?

I will never forget the day our yearbook came out in my freshman year of college. There was one particular guy, Keith, who had prided himself on his disinterest in the whole thing. While nearly every other student was looking over the yearbooks and signing them for friends, Keith told us he didn't care to buy one; he was totally apathetic about looking at stupid photos of the meaningless activities on campus that year. It was all so…childish and self-absorbed.

What made the whole episode funny is that while a bunch of us sat in the dining hall looking at the yearbooks, mine sat in front of Keith as he ate his lunch. It was just begging him to crack it open and look it over. Finally, when he thought no one was observing him, he opened up the yearbook and began leafing through it. Before long, he was on an intentional hunt for something in that book. I finally noticed and asked him: "Keith—what are you looking for?"

"Uh…nothing. I am just looking at pictures of my friends."

"Yeah, right!" we all said, laughing. Sure enough, when he arrived at the page he was searching for, there it was staring him in the face—his own mug shot, his senior picture…in full color. Everyone leaned over to see this apathetic student smile as he found himself in the "stupid" book. Needless to say, he was a source of comedy for us that day.

Keith, however, is a picture of another principle for communicators and advocates. We all know that regardless of what people say, when they open up their school yearbook, they are looking for their own photo. In fact, they want to see all the times the photographer took a snapshot of them that year on campus. Audiences listen to speakers the same way: They are looking for themselves in the talk. They want to know where they fit in. They are asking, *Does this subject have anything to do with me? Is it relevant to my life? Is there something for me to take away?*

Communicators and advocates fail when they get so wrapped up in the information they're transmitting, they forget that people are tuned in to W.I.I.F.M. Radio: What's In It For Me? If we prioritize information above translation into the lives of our listeners, they may just check out mentally. Especially in our noisy, cluttered culture, we must help people translate and apply information to their personal lives. As communicators, we must understand that most people, including you and me, have a unique, often self-serving agenda. (This isn't necessarily bad, because it helps us achieve our goals and protect ourselves.) We cannot assume that someone will know or share our agenda when we speak. Communicators must discover what's most important to their listeners in order to know how to approach their subject. According to author Tim Sanders, audiences will give you red lights and green lights with their body language. Communicators and advocates must look for these signals to know if they're connecting. Can you see from their faces that they identify with you? "If you can find a way to be relevant to someone else, you get a green light and can drive on. Otherwise, the light stays red. That smiling, sweet doorman may be the friendliest man you've ever met, but if your building is across the street from his and you have no contact with him, you don't really care whether he's friendly."[18]

Questions to Ask Yourself

As you prepare your comments before you speak as an agriculture communicator and advocate, try asking these questions:

1. Why should a person listen to this message?

2. Does it involve them at an emotional level?

3. Will this message matter tomorrow as they begin their day?

4. Can each person practice the big idea?

5. Is this message concrete enough to be useful?

6. How could someone apply this message to his or her life?

These questions are great guides as you prepare to be relevant to an audience. Now, here is my question for you: Do you focus on being interesting or interested? Seth Godin differentiates these two ideas brilliantly. He talks about the difference between interesting and interested.[19] Most of us want to be interesting to people. When we say something, we want others to perk up and listen.

We want to have influence by having good content. It turns out that the best way to appear interesting to someone who cares a lot about himself is to be interested…in him. Let's be honest. If you are not that interested in what your audience is thinking about, it might be you'll be less interesting to them.

Jim Rohn once said, "The goal of effective communication should be for listeners to say, 'Me too!' versus 'So what?'"

Market managers for Farmers Markets practice this principle all the time. Farmers markets have grown in popularity over the past few decades and now there are many products and services that go way beyond simply fruits and vegetables. At the Green City Market in Chicago, customers can take advantage of numerous educational programs to learn about specific agricultural topics that interest them. The Farmers Market in Los Angeles offers musical performances two nights a week to entertain their customers with appealing music in addition to the food. Pike Place Market in Seattle realized that people shopping for food were also interested in arts and crafts, so they added kiosks featuring local artwork. In each instance, these markets listened to what their customers wanted and found ways to provide it.

David Burns, a medical doctor and professor of psychiatry at the University of Pennsylvania, observed, "The biggest mistake you can make in trying to talk convincingly is to put your highest priority on expressing your own ideas and feelings. What most people really want is to be listened to, respected and understood. The moment people see that they are being understood, they become motivated to understand your point of view."[20] John Maxwell taught me: "If you can learn to understand people—how they think, what they feel, what inspires them, how they're likely to act in a given situation—then you can motivate and influence them in a positive way."

Perhaps another way to say this is simply: Once people find their own picture in the yearbook, they'll soon want to find yours as well.

Talk It Over

1. An audience gives a speaker red lights or green lights by their body language. What are some examples of each that you've encountered when you have given a speech or had a conversation about agriculture?

   _____

   _____

2. What causes an individual to move from "So what?" to "Me too!"? How does self-interest capture the listener's attention?

   _____

   _____

3. What are some practical ways that you can help people find their own picture in the yearbook, especially if they don't have a background in agriculture or readily understand how it is relevant to their daily lives?

_____

_____

4. What is the primary difference between being interesting and being interested? How do you show your audience that you are focused on being interested rather than interesting?

_____

_____

Self Assessment

Use the following questions to assess yourself on how relevant your communication is. Mark an "X" in the space that best describes your current application of this principle.

1. What do you focus on more when you're communicating with others?

   Interesting to them _ _ _ _ _ _ _ _ _ _ _ _ _ _ _ Interested in them

2. Based on past audience feedback, what response do your talks often elicit?

   So what? _ Me, too!

3. As you prepare to communicate, do you tend to focus more on the abstract or personal?

   Abstract _ Personal

Try It Out

Sit down with a team of people and discuss a global agricultural need or issue such as climate change or food insecurity. Then, based on this *Habitude*, practice pitching why people should be interested and get involved regarding this particular issue. How can they answer the question, "What's in it for me?"

As you begin this exercise, think through the following:

- The details of the audience: Are they married or single? Rich or poor? Elderly or young? Farmers or non-farmers? Familiar with agriculture and FFA or not?

- The personality of the audience members: Are they passionate? Reflective? Relational?

- Why wouldn't they want to get involved: Are they busy with other tasks? Lack of interest? Misperceptions about the issue?

The Paul Revere Principle

PAUL REVERE AND WILLIAM DAWES BOTH MADE A MIDNIGHT RIDE, BUT ONLY ONE WAS ABLE TO CONNECT WITH AND INFLUENCE PEOPLE. THE TEST OF AN ADVOCATE'S CREDIBILITY LIES IN HIS OR HER ABILITY TO MOBILIZE OTHERS.

Just outside of Boston on April 18th, 1775, a young stable boy overheard two British soldiers talking. They hinted of an attack on the colonists in New England, and they said something about the townsmen having "hell to pay" tomorrow. The young boy ran to inform a silversmith by the name of Paul Revere. After careful thought, Revere determined to mobilize the area against the attack the British were planning. And the rest, as they say, is history.

Paul Revere made his famous "midnight ride," which actually began about 10:00 p.m. that night. He raced on horseback through the towns and villages surrounding Boston, challenging locals to get up and defend their country! By the next morning, as the Redcoats secretly made their way inland, they were met in Lexington by a huge group of volunteers, American patriots. They were shocked, to say the least. The British were unprepared and outdone that morning—and the Revolutionary War was underway.

An interesting bit of trivia from this story is that Paul Revere wasn't the only Patriot to make a midnight ride. A tanner by the name of William Dawes also took the ride. He rode on a similar horse, covered a similar amount of territory and carried an identical message, but Dawes had difficulty getting anyone to act. In fact, he was so poor at mobilizing folks, historians assumed for years Dawes must have traveled to pro-British towns. But, alas, he hadn't. He simply lacked the capability to mobilize people, even for a cause they agreed with.

This contrast illustrates another important advocacy principle. I call it the "Paul Revere Principle." When you boil down the essence of communication and advocacy to its bare minimum, it's about mobilizing others to act. Paul Revere was able to connect with and influence townspeople to get up and respond. William Dawes, on the other hand, couldn't get one single man to even turn over in bed!

(Well—that may be a bit of an exaggeration.) For some reason, though, Dawes lacked the credibility, communication skills, aptitude, trust and respect to move people toward taking a risk.

So what is it, then, that enables a communicator and advocate to motivate people to action? There are many answers to that question, but let me suggest a few:

1. INSIGHT – People listen to you because of what you know.
   Example: Ben Franklin. Ben influenced people through his knowledge, wisdom and insight.

2. RELATIONSHIPS – People listen because of who you know.
   Example: Ambassador Kenneth Quinn. He is the president of the World Food Prize Foundation, leveraging his extensive connections to combat hunger around the world.

3. SACRIFICE – People listen because of what you've suffered.
   Example: Mother Teresa. Harvard grads and U.S. presidents listened because of her sacrificial life.

4. ABILITIES – People listen because of what you are able to do.
   Example: Judy Olson was the first female president of the Washington Association of Wheat Growers (WAWG), and she has been the Washington State Director of USDA's Farm Service Agency since 2009. She has proven that she can do the job.

5. EXPERIENCE – People listen because of what you've achieved.
   Example: Temple Grandin rose above limitations of autism to be a pioneer and advocate for animal handling and care.

6. INTUITION – People listen because of what you sense.
   Example: Thomas Edison and Steve Jobs. They saw a new world coming before the rest of us did.

7. CHARACTER – People listen because of your integrity.
   Example: Abraham Lincoln. In 1935, his partner William Berry, died suddenly and left Lincoln with a large amount of debt. Through hard work, Lincoln not only paid the debts of the business, but also the personal debts of the family Berry left behind. The character he established in his youth prepared him to become the kind of person a whole nation could learn to follow.

8. HUMILITY – People listen because of your heart.
   Example: Botanist Norman Borlaug looked at the world and saw a problem. Population was increasing and millions were starving every year in third world countries. Instead of a global campaign or a food drive, Borlaug developed a disease resistant, high-yield, wheat varieties that are still in use today. He changed the world in his own quiet way.

9. RELEVANCE – People listen because you identify with their needs.
   Example: Martin Luther King, Jr. He identified with common folks; he marched and bled with them.

10. CONVICTIONS – People listen because of your passion.
   Example: Robert Fraley. He is recognized as the father of agricultural biotechnology and remains passionate about discovering new technologies that support farmers.

Let me ask you a question: Why do people listen to you? What reasons do you give them to follow you? Good communicators and advocates find a way to connect with people. They earn their right to be followed. They build bridges of relationship that can bear the weight of truth.

You may be familiar with the name Malala Yousufzai. She is an 18 year old from Pakistan who has become an unlikely communicator and advocate for women and children around the world. Malala's father ran a public school and believed that young girls had a right to get an education. In 2009, Malala began writing an anonymous blog for the BBC expressing her views on education—even though she lived under the daily threat of the Taliban taking over the region of the country where her family lived.

Malala continued to speak out even when she and her father began to get death threats. After the BBC blog ended, a documentary was made about her life. It named her as the author of the BBC blog, and she received international attention. In 2012, she received Pakistan's first National Youth Peace Prize and her public profile continued to grow. However, this also caused the Taliban to see her as a more dangerous threat to their cause and they decided to take action. They voted to kill her.

On October 9, 2012, a masked gunman boarded the bus Malala was riding and called for her by name. He shot her with a single bullet that penetrated her head, neck, and shoulder. For months she received intensive medical treatment and miraculously she survived, despite all of the odds against her.

This shooting incident and Malala's refusal to back down on her beliefs thrust her into a even stronger position to fight for the rights of millions of children around the world who are denied an education. She started The Malala Fund which helps to raise awareness of the impact for girls to be educated and further, to give young women a voice.

Malala's courage and perseverance have given her a platform that has allowed her to mobilize people all over the world to take action. I'd say she is a modern day Paul Revere.

TALK IT OVER

Communicators and advocates must earn the right to be heard and followed. This chapter opened with the example of Paul Revere's ability to connect with and influence the townspeople to action. After his story, I listed ten reasons that enable leaders to motivate people to action.

1. Using that list, reflect on why people should listen to what you have to say about agricultural issues. Which reasons are true about your influence with people? Why should people listen to you?

_____

_____

2. Who is an agriculture leader you admire? Why do you believe what he or she says? What qualities does this leader have that you want to emulate?

_____

_____

SELF ASSESSMENT

This chapter contained a list of 10 ways a communicator and an advocate can motivate people to take action. Review this list and then determine two or three that you would like to focus on to improve your advocacy.

1. INSIGHT – People listen to you because of what you know.

2. RELATIONSHIPS – People listen because of who you know.

3. SACRIFICE – People listen because of what you've suffered.

4. ABILITIES – People listen because of what you are able to do.

5. EXPERIENCE – People listen because of what you've achieved.

6. INTUITION – People listen because of what you sense.

7. CHARACTER – People listen because of your integrity.

8. HUMILITY – People listen because of your heart.

9. RELEVANCE – People listen because you identify with their needs.

10. CONVICTIONS – People listen because of your passion.

In the mid 1800's, John Deere moved to Illinois to make a new life for himself. Working as a blacksmith, he noticed that the pioneer farmers were having trouble plowing the thick mid-western soil with their plows that were designed in New England. Mr. Deere listened to the farmers around him, and created just the plow they needed. He obtained their respect and admiration by meeting their needs. Years later, once he had created a thriving business, he approached the same community that he had helped transform. Now a politician, they elected him Mayor for two terms. The credibility that he earned as a business man, aided him later in his political aspirations.

Thinking of John Deere's example, how you can follow in his footsteps and earn credibility from those around you? Discuss the following questions with your group:

1. Think of an agricultural issue that you want your community to care about. What could you do for your community to earn the right to be heard about the issue you really think is critical?

_____

_____

2. What are specific action steps you could take to begin building a platform to share your views?

_____

_____

Small Sprocket

COMMUNICATORS AND ADVOCATES ARE THE SMALL SPROCKETS IN EFFECTING CHANGE. WE MUST SPIN DOZENS OF TIMES BEFORE THE BIG GEAR MAKES ONE REVOLUTION. IT'S PART OF THE TERRITORY. SPIN LIKE CRAZY AND EVENTUALLY OTHERS WILL RESPOND.

As a high school student, I rode my bike to school—at least until I got a car. Riding my bike was memorable because I had to ride up a huge hill called "Fletcher Parkway." It was a solid, three-quarter mile, uphill climb. Every morning, I was sweating by the time I reached the top. Thanks, Schwinn, for your ten-speed bikes! Shifting into low gear was my only hope. (As you know, low gears allow a biker to climb hills when there's no momentum). My trade-off was pedaling like crazy just to move a few feet.

I suppose it's a little like a car. When you drive, the engine revs between 1,000 and 3,000 RPMs (revolutions per minute), depending on the momentum you have. In other words, a car's motor spins thousands of revolutions each moment, only to move your tires down the road just one, short mile! It's a small wheel moving a big wheel—a tiny gear spinning frantically, to move the larger one just a bit. It's the Law of Leverage…and it illustrates the principle of the Small Sprocket.

Imagine two sprockets. One small one, one big one. It's the job of the small sprocket to turn the big sprocket. If the small sprocket is half the size of the big one, it must go around twice before the big one completes a full revolution. Doesn't sound too bad, does it? Now imagine that small sprocket is 100th the size of the big one. Now it must rotate 100 times in order to make the big sprocket complete a full revolution!

That's how life is for the leader of an organization or a successful communicator and advocate. Sometimes things flow smoothly and you don't feel like you're working too hard. Then there are times (and these are more common) when you have to work, work, work, work, work—just to feel like you are progressing at all! You spin and spin and spin in order to accomplish all of your tasks. You keep communicating the vision, but everyone still seems fuzzy on it. You equip others to advocate for an issue, but you still at times feel like a one-man or one-woman show. You labor and labor…anticipating seeing some result.

It can be discouraging. Sometimes, it feels like you've moved ahead fifty miles, but other times it seems as if your progress is moving like an inchworm! How can this be?

Relax. It's normal. Welcome to leadership and communication. Leaders must spin like a small sprocket to get the larger group to spin just once. It can be tiresome. At first, the labor ratio is often disproportionate. But just wait. Continue spinning. Good news is coming. People will eventually respond to your spinning. And you know what? Once you really get moving and have the group responding positively, that big sprocket starts picking up speed from its own momentum. In time, the group will be spinning you!

Back in 2000, a movie came out called *Pay It Forward*. Based on a true story, Trevor McKinney creates the "pay it forward" idea as a social studies project in school. The breakdown is pretty simple: do something to help someone, then ask them to do the same for three other individuals. Don't pay the kindness back; pay it forward. The whole movie is about Trevor helping people and trying to inspire them to pay it forward. His project seems to be failing, as Trevor spins and spins…and nobody seems to join his quest to make the world a better place. He is ready to give up.

In the end, Trevor learns that he started a movement. From homeless people to corporate chief executive officers (CEOs), his good deeds and their forward momentum reached so many people that they caught the attention of a reporter. The truth is, Trevor had been spinning a long time before he saw any results. In his eyes, the big sprocket hadn't moved. But in reality, it was actually just picking up momentum. Hearing that his project was successful re-ignited Trevor's original desire to share kindness in the world. In the movie, there were increased random acts of kindness throughout the region. In real life, however, the movie inspired the creation of the "Pay It Forward" movement. People are paying it forward from Washington to Florida, all the way to Singapore and Australia.

In 1809, a boy named Louie was born in a small town near Paris. His early years consisted of many difficult obstacles. Playing with his father's tools one day, Louie pierced and destroyed his left eye. Shortly after that, his damaged eye infected the other, causing complete loss of sight in both eyes. While most blind people at the time became beggars, Louie wanted to attend school. So at the age of ten, he enrolled in a school for the blind. Students were taught to read raised letters, but due to the difficult process, only 14 books were available to study. Louie knew there had to be an easier way and set about creating a finger alphabet.

He began creating a system that would allow every blind person to read, write and communicate. Early on, it had little success because the system was too complex for kids to master. But Louie experimented with more simplified systems over the next few months, finally arriving at the ideal "six dot" system. By the time he was fifteen, Louie had developed separate codes for math and music.

Although his creation had improved life for blind people, it didn't catch on. Sighted people didn't understand how the dot system could be useful. One teacher even banned children from learning it.

Eventually—after years of spinning like crazy—folks realized the benefits of the system. Today, the Braille System has been adapted to almost every known language, from Albanian to Zulu. Against all odds, Louie became an independent man and even went on to become a teacher in his old school.

As a young leader, I remember trying to start new projects in the organization where I was employed. I thought my ideas were great, but few others agreed. After all, I was the new kid on the block and I was young. Fortunately, there were a few of us who began spinning like small sprockets. We knew we couldn't spin wildly in all directions, so we consistently spun like crazy in one direction. I'd look in the mirror each day and say, "I'm a small sprocket!" Over time, momentum picked up. Management saw that our ideas had potential, and we were given the go ahead to begin implementing some of them. By the time I left that job, we were successful in reaching all of our original goals.

We were small sprockets. As leaders, if we don't have the courage and determination to keep spinning, things will grind to a halt. Very little will change. In fact, the vision will shrivel and the team will likely suffer. It's the leader's job to spin like crazy and fire up the rest of the team. It's part of the territory of advocacy. Fueled by determination, advocates are the engines. We are the small sprockets.

TALK IT OVER

In the world of nature, we can learn a lot about the small sprocket principle from the ant, a small creature. Their highly organized colonies often consist of millions of individual ants, yet they appear to operate as a single entity. They work in teams to move extremely heavy things. They gather food during harvest and store it until the winter months arrive. Without an administrator, they perform specific jobs as workers, soldiers, drones and queens. Yet, when a catastrophe occurs, the ants quickly adapt their duties to overcome the problem.

1. Summarize the characteristics that enable the ant to succeed:

_____

_____

2. Contrast the ant's initiative and perseverance with our own human laziness. Why do we often fail to persevere? What prevents our "spinning?"

_____

_____

3. How does this principle specifically impact you as an agriculture communicator and advocate?

_____

_____

SELF ASSESSMENT

Evaluate yourself on the following three qualities that we find in an ant's work ethic.

1. INTEGRITY: The ant doesn't need supervision. It works because it is the right thing to do. Have you ever been in a program that seemed motionless? What kept it from making progress?

_____

_____

2. INITIATIVE: The ant starts to gather food without being pushed. It doesn't need someone to show it the way. In your activities, do you ever feel alone in doing all the work? How do you typically respond?

_____

_____

3. INDUSTRY: The ant has a spirit of industry. It works and works until the job is done. How do you stay inspired when you don't see results and you don't feel any gratification?

_____

_____

TRY IT OUT

Choose an issue or agricultural cause that you believe needs to be promoted in your classroom, school or in your FFA chapter. Determine to take six months and actively promote this cause. Choose two or three actions you can take that would strategically help your fellow classmates and community members understand and support the cause. Then—do them. Spin like crazy. Evaluate at the end of six months.

- Do you see any improvement? Will it take more time?

_____

_____

Or, organize a team of fellow members to compete with you at one of the Career Development Events (CDE). Set a timeline and develop an action plan. You may need to plan up to a year in advance to get it right. Then, choose to practice this *Habitude*. Evaluate your progress in 6 to 12 months.

[End Notes]

1. Ellen McGirt, "I Want My Twitter TV!" Fast Company, December/January 2010–2011. http://www.fastcompany.com/node/1702772/print

2. Donald Miller, A Million Miles in a Thousand Years: What I Learned While Editing My Life, (Nashville, TN: Thomas Nelson, 2009).

3. David Brooks, The Social Animal: The Hidden Sources of Love, Character, and Achievement, (New York, NY: Random House, 2011), 338.

4. James C. Humes, The Sir Winston Method: The Five Secrets of Speaking the Language of Leadership, (New York, NY: W. Morrow, 1991).

5. Chip Heath and Dan Heath, Made to Stick: Why Some Ideas Survive and Others Die, (New York, NY: Random House, 2007), 33–34.

6. Malcolm Gladwell, The Tipping Point: How Little Things Can Make a Big Difference, (Boston, MA: Little, Brown, 2000), 96–97.

7. Chip Heath and Dan Heath, Made to Stick: Why Some Ideas Survive and Others Die, (New York, NY: Random House, 2007), 19–20.

8. Brad Lomenick and Ralph Winter, "Interview with Ralph Winter," November 11, 2010. http://vimeo.com/16747532

9. Mark Turner, The Literary Mind, (New York, NY: Oxford University Press, 1996), 4–5.

10. Donald Miller, "Living a Good Story, an Alternative to New Years Resolutions," Donald Miller's Blog, January 1, 2010. http://donmilleris.com/ 2010/01/01/living-a-good-story-an-alternative-to-new-years-resolutions/

11. Malcolm Gladwell, The Tipping Point: How Little Things Can Make a Big Difference, (Boston, MA: Little, Brown, 2000), 98.

12. Sean D'Souza, "Why Urgency Succeeds Like Nothing Else in a Bad Economy," Copyblogger. http://www.copyblogger.com/urgency-bad-economy/

13. Chip Bell and Bilijack Bell, Magnetic Service: Secrets of Creating Passionately Devoted Customers (San Francisco, CA: Berrett-Koehler Publishers, 2003)

14. Lubell, Sam. "No Pink Slip. You're Just Dot-Gone." New York Times 150, no. 51696 (03/18/2001):

15. Doris Kearns Goodwin, "The Master of the Game," Time, July 2005, vol. 166.

16. Robert S. McNamara with Brian VanDeMark, In Retrospect: The Tragedy and Lessons of Vietnam (New York: Vintage, 1996)

17. James C. Humes, The Sir Winston Method: The Five Secrets of Speaking the Language of Leadership, (New York, NY: W. Morrow, 1991), 24.

18. Tim Sanders, The Likeability Factor: How to Boost Your L-Factor & Achieve Your Life's Dreams, (New York, NY: Crown Publishers, 2005), 98–99.

19. Seth Godin, "Interesting & Interested," July 24, 2011. http://sethgodin.typepad.com/seths_blog/2011/07/interesting-interested.html

20. John C. Maxwell and Jim Dornan, Becoming a Person of Influence, (Nashville, TN: Maxwell Motivation, 1997), 100 –101.

[Supplemental Resources]

MOVIES

- The Social Network. Dir. David Fincher. Sony Pictures. 2010. Film.
- Pay It Forward. Dir. Mimi Leder. Warner Bros. Pictures. 2000. Film.

BOOKS

- Miller, Donald. A Million Miles in a Thousand Years. Thomas Nelson. 2011. Print.
- Pink, Daniel. Drive: The Surprising Truth About What Motivates Us. Riverhead Books. 2011. Print.
- Brooks, David. The Social Animal: The Hidden Sources of Love, Character, and Achievement. Random House. 2012. Print.
- Heath, Chip. Made to Stick: Why Some Ideas Survive and Others Die. Random House. 2007. Print.
- Turner, Mark. The Literary Mind: The Origins of Thought and Language. Oxford University Press. 1998.
- Bell, Chip. Magnetic Service: Secrets for Creating Passionately Devoted Customers. Berrett-Koehler Publishers. 2006.
- McNamara, Robert. In Retrospect: The Tragedy and Lessons of Vietnam. Vintage Books. 1996.

Acknowledgments

This page is a "thank you" note. Like any book project, this one represents the collaboration of many people who shared the same goal—to assemble a set of *Habitudes* that spark conversation and action among those who read it.

First, I want to thank my friend, Josh Bledsoe, who saw the vision for this book immediately and had the courage to ask: "Why not?"

Thank you Seth Harden, Ambra Tennery and Christine White for being the "boots on the ground" team members at the national FFA office, who worked to ensure the customization for this book was in place. I appreciate your labor of love.

Thanks to Holly Moore, vice president at Growing Leaders, who undertook the major edits and "tailoring" necessary so that this book met the goal of developing leaders and advocates among the students who explore it. It was heavy lifting.

Thanks to Hannah Pratt, who led this project, coordinating the communication between Growing Leaders and the national FFA office and organizing the revisions. We needed you to help coordinate the team's efforts along the way. Thanks for your kind spirit as you pushed this project forward.

Thanks to J.T. Thoms—Mr. Energy—who fostered this partnership between Growing Leaders and FFA, and made sure it was a win/win opportunity for both. Your people skills and vision are priceless. Thanks for using them so well.

Thank you Jim Woodard, who oversaw the layout and formatting of this manuscript. You are always an unsung hero, who never calls attention to himself. You simply get the job done quietly yet exquisitely. I am grateful for you every day.

Thank you Anne Alexander, my long-time comrade and editor, who's shared so many book projects with me and actually still enjoys the journey. Your gifts, Anne, play a vital role in every written project. You make us better.

Finally, thanks to Andrew McPeak, who stepped in and added value, like he always does when he's involved in a project. His "words gifts" and intuition are extraordinary. Thanks Andrew for being a Millennial who understands how to speak to students.

Team efforts are hard, but definitely worth it. I am grateful for you all.

[Notes]

[Notes]